✔ KU-785-390

RANGERS

PACKED WITH INFORMATION ON THE GERS

This edition published and distributed by Parragon, 1998

Parragon
Unit 13-17 Avonbridge Trading Estate
Atlantic Road
Avonmouth
Bristol BS11 9QD

Produced by Magpie Books,
an imprint of Robinson Publishing Ltd, London

ISBN 0 75252 549 2

A copy of the British Library Cataloguing–in–Publication
Data is available from the British Library.

Printed and bound in the EC.

This independent publication has been prepared without any
involvement on the part of Rangers Football Club or the
Scottish Premier League.

RANGERS

PACKED WITH INFORMATION ON THE GERS

John Scott

P

· PARRAGON ·

CONTENTS

INTRODUCTION

In a city where football is more than just a pastime, Glasgow Rangers, founded in 1873, have always considered themselves the senior of the two major powers. When the ninth consecutive Championship, registered in 1997, brought them level with their local rivals, the stakes were raised even higher. Yet, no matter what silverware resides at Ibrox at any given time, the club is an institution.

And that institution has been built by the characters that have brought it success. Players like Alan Morton, George Young, Jim Baxter, John Greig, Richard Gough and Ally McCoist have kept Rangers in the hunt for national and international honours, managers like Willie Waddell, Bill Struth, Walter Smith and Jock Wallace guiding the club's fortunes through the years.

By dividing Rangers' history into easily digestible sections, this book seeks to inform and entertain. It cannot by its very size be exhaustive, and it is hoped that anyone fascinated by the facts and figures will purchase one of the weighty club histories available or follows Rangers' match-by-match progress through the *Rothmans Football Yearbook*, published annually.

In these pages, however, you'll find details of the great players and double acts, the managers profiled together with their achievements, quotes, statistics, dream teams, month-by-month milestones…in short, much of what has gone to make this club a football institution.

GOALS GALORE!

When it comes to goals and Glasgow Rangers, some would say the only name you need to know is Alastair McCoist...

Well, that's not strictly true. After all, Marco Negri the Italian scoring machine has fast imprinted his name and rugged likeness on the hearts and minds of the Ibrox faithful — and let's not forget Bob McPhail, whose career from 1926 to 1940 established a 233-goal record that would last well over half a century until 'Super Ally' eclipsed it in 1996.

The Scottish League kicked off in 1890-91, and Rangers' campaign opened with three excellent wins out of four — 5-2, 6-2 and 8-2. Unfortunately the third game of the four was a 5-1 defeat by Dumbarton! They'd eventually share the title with the Sons, a play–off game intended to decide the title ending a very even 2-2. Top scorer in Rangers' first two League seasons was John 'Kitey' McPherson, a player so versatile he turned out in every jersey including the goalkeeper's in his dozen years with the club. Little wonder this goalpoacher later became a director!

Rangers' biggest ever win came in the Scottish FA Cup –
14-2 against Blairgowrie in the first round of 1934. Two
seasons before that, Sam English had created the club's League
goalscoring record for a season with 44, a figure that still
stands (though Marco Negri clearly has designs on it: watch
this space!).

Bob McPhail also stayed on at Ibrox after he hung up his
shooting boots, as reserve-team trainer, but while a player his
lethal left-wing combination with winger Alan Morton saw
him frequently getting himself on the end of some pinpoint
crosses. With 230 League goals, plus three in war games and
another 70 with former club Airdrie, it was a surprise that he
gained a meagre 17 international caps in Scotland's darker
blue.

Perhaps the most significant single goal scored by a Ranger
came from Derek Johnstone in 1970 when his strike won new
manager Willie Waddell his first silverware, the League Cup.
Johnstone, who'd go on to score 209 goals in 547 career
games for the Gers, was still a matter of days short of his
seventeenth birthday, and the fact that it won the game against
Old Firm rivals Celtic made the goal even sweeter! Lisbon
Lions Billy McNeill and Jim Craig couldn't stop his powerful
header, and the result was an instant legend.

RANGERS

The name of Stein means different things to different halves of Glasgow. The blue side will immediately recognise Colin, a centre-forward in the tall, strong, target-man mould who will forever be remembered as one of the goalscorers when Rangers brought home the Cup Winners' Cup from Barcelona in 1972 – still, amazingly, their last European silverware. Such was the respect in which Colin was held that, like Derek Johnstone, he returned to Ibrox for a second spell after trying his luck south of the border with Coventry. His 21 Scotland appearances brought ten goals, confirming him as a netbuster of the highest class.

John Greig isn't remembered as a goalscorer, but the final act of his five years as manager was to sign Ally McCoist from Sunderland. He was hardly an overnight success, new manager Jock Wallace suggesting he might like to return to Roker in quick style, but he fought on and he turned in a leading scorer's total every season: figures of 35, 25, 41 (twice), 49 and 25 saw him undisputed goal king of Ibrox until Mo Johnston took his crown for just one campaign.

This cheeky act spurred McCoist to even greater heights, and in 1991-92 he swept the board, notching his 200th Scottish League strike, Rangers' 100th goal of the season and won the European Golden Boot honour with 41 goals. If that was good, the next season made history as he became the first player ever to retain the Golden Boot, 34 goals in as many League games.

There are few easy games these days, no matter what the cynics may say, so Rangers only went 'nap' twice in their ninth consecutive Championship–winning season of 1996–97 – against Dunfermline and Motherwell – though they also hit Raith for six in the final month. Best individual performers were hat-trick heroes McCoist, Gascoigne and Andersen. But now, with Marco Negri intent on bursting every net he can find, it could be time to write a new chapter in the record books...

THROUGH THE YEARS
JANUARY

1956
January
28

After hitting the target on 23 occasions, normally deadly left-winger John Hubbard fails to net a Rangers penalty. Fortunately, Rangers beat Airdrie 4–0 anyway, Hubbard scoring from open play.

1985
January
19

Aberdeen beat Rangers at Pittodrie to administer the club's first and only five-goal thrashing since the Premier League was first established. The warning sign was more than ominous: the Dons finished top with 59 points, Rangers fourth with 38.

1967
January
28

Berwick Rangers' shock 1-0 Cup win over Rangers makes worldwide headlines. Little wonder: it was the first time Rangers had fallen at the first hurdle for 30 years and the first time in the century to a club from outside the top division.

1971
January
2

While Ne'erday (New Year's Day) games with Celtic have a history all their own, this one had a lethal sting in the tail – fans leaving the stadium tried to return on hearing a late goal scored, Stairway 13 crumbled and carnage ensued. A total of 66 died and 145 were injured.

1997
January
2

It's that man Andersen again! Fresh from a pre-Christmas hat-trick, his introduction as a substitute swung the crucial New Year match against Celtic. The game was balanced at 1–1 before Andersen was brought into play: his two crucial goals handed Rangers a points advantage the Parkhead side ultimately couldn't overhaul.

DREAM TEAM 1

First and foremost in the Ibrox roll of honour is the team that turned Rangers' long-cherished European dream into reality in Barcelona in 1972.

14

Goalkeeper **Peter McCloy**

Towering keeper who commanded his defence and was to be ever-present in all competitions of the 1971–72 season. Three European clean sheets, all at home, helped the cause considerably.

Right-back **Sandy Jardine**

Reliable full-back, cool under pressure and comfortable on the ball, who weighed in with a handy goal to see off Bayern Munich. Went on to become a legend all over again at Hearts after over 650 games in a blue shirt.

Left-back **Willie Mathieson**

Missed few games at left-back and was ever-present in Cup competitions. No attacking inclinations to speak of, but a doughty defender who took few prisoners.

Right-half **John Greig**

A stalwart captain and future Rangers manager who led by example. His absence through injury (he was back for the European Final) played a large part in the side finishing only third in the League.

RANGERS

Centre-half   Derek Johnstone

Marked Bayern Munich dangerman Hoeness out of the Semi-Finals after a season in which he was as much out of the side than in. Preferred this position, centre-half, to the forward role he started his Rangers career in.

Left-half   Dave Smith

Canny sweeper, playing in place of the injured McKinnon, who created both Rangers' first two Final goals with deep balls from defence.

Outside-right   Tommy McLean

A recent recruit from Kilmarnock, five-foot-four Tommy fought off competition from Willie Henderson for the shirt to become a major part of the Rangers story, playing nearly 450 games for the club.

Inside-right   Alfie Conn

Midfield schemer, then just 20 and full of promise, who also played for Celtic after a spell south of the border with Spurs. Despite two caps in 1975, his international career failed to blossom as it appeared it would in '72.

Centre-forward   **Colin Stein**

A classic old-fashioned centre-forward who led the line well and was top European scorer with five goals from nine games. In the first of two separate spells at Ibrox, having cost a record £100,000 from Hibs in 1968.

Inside-left   **Alex McDonald**

Scored a couple of crucial European goals in the first leg and Quarter-Finals that saw Rangers past difficult opposition. At £50,000, his 500-plus games for Rangers in all competitions cost peanuts.

Outside-left   **Willie Johnston**

Two goals in the Final, the first a rare header, gave this talented yet temperamental player a pre-eminent place in the Rangers European roll of honour.

APPEARANCES

In the old days, the characters who 'played for the shirt' often stayed with the shirt.

The advent of the Bosman ruling was the final nail in the coffin as far as appearance records go, and it's far more likely that crowds will enjoy the skills of a star player for two, maybe three seasons before they look to better their pay packet, if not their status, elsewhere. With loyalty at a premium, little wonder Richard Gough was summoned back from the US to add to his 508 League appearances and help Rangers out of an injury crisis. Despite his impressive total of games, though, he's far from the Top 10 of appearances in a blue shirt. Only Ally McCoist of the 1990s Rangers makes it.

Top of the list in League terms are right-back Dougie Gray and winger Sandy Archibald, both of whom played the majority of their games in the inter-war period. Gray rates at 667 and Archibald 514…unless you discount Gray's 177 wartime games, which puts him two dozen behind his 'rival'. Archibald started in 1916-17, but as explained elsewhere Scottish football played on through the First World War.

John Greig and Sandy Jardine of the classic Cup Winners' Cup line-up both make it into the League appearance listings as third (498) and fifth (451) respectively. Greig played all his career in a blue shirt, while Jardine would become the first Scottish player to pass the thousand mark, in all first-class competitions, while with Hearts. Splitting them is David Meiklejohn, one of the club's great captains, with 490.

Then come Tommy Cairns (1913-27, 407), George Young (1941-57, 403 including 110 wartime) Alex Smith (1893-1915, 402) and Alan Morton (1920-33, 382) before we get to

Ally McCoist. His total of League games, 403 to end 1996-97, has of course been accompanied by the Rangers goal record – though yet again if wartime figures were allowed to count, Jimmy Smith's 300 goals would be top of the pile.

Turning our attention to players who've done well in individual seasons, it would be hard to beat the record of the so-called 'Iron Curtain' defence on which Rangers built their immediate postwar success. Keeper Bobby Brown was ever-present in 1946-47, and all the way through to the final game of the 1951-52 season. In 1948-49, the 'back six' missed only six games between them, in 1949-50 just two. If you consider injuries and suspension, especially the latter given the players' defensive duties, it's a particularly impressive record.

In the early days of the Souness reign, players like Chris Woods, McCoist and Davie Cooper recorded 40-plus totals in a 46-game Premier League, while, in shades of the Iron Curtain, the 1991-92 team saw Numbers 1-3 and 5 – Goram, Stevens, Robertson and Spackman – drop just five games between them. Gough at 4 let the side down in relative terms with 'just' 33. One of the unluckiest players of the era was midfielder Lee Robertson, who made just one League appearance in three of the four seasons between 1991 and 1995 but could never make the breakthrough.

Several recent foreign stars have played relatively rarely after the fanfare of a high-priced arrival. Basile Boli's brief sojourn, soured by indiscreet comments that filtered back from his native France, has already been referred to, while South American ace Seb Rozental injured himself almost immediately on arrival.

Aside from injury, another bugbear for today's players to cope with is an ever-growing international fixture list that will often see stars withdrawn from domestic action to play for their countries. It's something the Rangers squad is likely to suffer more and more as time goes on unless some concerted action is taken by FIFA.

THROUGH THE YEARS
FEBRUARY

1872

February

This was the month Rangers was formed by a group of students: the club's name was borrowed from an English rugby outfit.

1894

February

17

Rangers today laid hands for the first time on the Scottish Cup, having beaten rivals Celtic 3-1 in the Final. By 1997, they'd won the trophy 27 times and had been beaten Finalists on 16 occasions.

1963
February

Not one competitive game was played this month by Rangers as the Big Freeze kept football north of the border on hold. Only the Ne'erday game had taken place in January, so the fixture backlog kept the club busy till the end of May – but the League and Cup Double was nevertheless secured.

1969
February
22

Ibrox idol Brian Laudrup was born today in Vienna. Though Rangers paid Fiorentina just over £2 million for his services in 1994, he proved as good value as he had for previous clubs Brondby, Bayer Uerdingen, Bayern Munich, Fiorentina and AC Milan.

1997
February
23

Jorg Albertz, the tough-tackling German full-back, today notched his ninth goal of a satisfying season – and this despite sharing spot-kick duties with McCoist and Gascoigne. He had already proved remarkable value for the £4.5 million fee Walter Smith paid previous club SV Hamburg, and, despite rumours of a return home, would play on into 1997-98.

GREAT STRIKERS

The Ibrox faithful have always demanded graft, guts and, above all, goals. Here are the men who supplied them.

 ## WILLIE JOHNSTON

It is a shame that Willie Johnston will always be remembered for his lack of discipline as well as his awesome skills. Born in Glasgow on 19 December 1946, Johnston signed for Rangers in 1964 and made his debut that August against St Johnstone. His skills on the wing were obvious from the start and the speed with which he could run with the ball was positively alarming for opposing full-backs. It wasn't long before this club form was recognised and Willie quickly made his way into the Scottish side, collecting a total of 22 caps.

Johnston also had an eye for goal and scored over 100 in his career, but the most important came in 1972. He scored two goals in the European Cup Winners' Cup Final as Rangers beat Moscow Dynamo 3-2 in Barcelona. He also collected one Scottish Cup and two League Cup medals.

His honours would have been far more numerous had he managed to control his temperament, but manager Jock Wallace grew tired of his antics (he was sent off 20 times in his career) and he left Rangers in 1972 just before the team entered their heyday.

He moved to West Brom and his form at the Hawthorns

re-established him to the extent that he regularly played for Scotland. That was until the Word Championships in 1978 when Willie was banned from international football for the rest of his career for failing a drug test. Shortly after this he left the Baggies and played in Vancouver for a spell before finally returning to Rangers in 1980.

He enjoyed two more seasons at Ibrox before moving on to Hearts and Falkirk, and did well in that time. He had the misfortune to play for the club immediately before and after they had enjoyed some of their greatest success – yet there can be no denying that when Willie Johnston managed to stay on the pitch the skill he produced was a joy to behold.

WILLIE JOHNSTON RANGERS RECORD 1964-72, 1980-81									
League		FA Cup		League Cup		Europe		Total	
Apps	Goals	Apps	Goals	Apps	Goals	Apps	Goals	Apps	Goals
246	91	42	10	74	16	40	8	402	125

 # DEREK JOHNSTONE

Born on 4 November 1953, Derek Johnstone moved to Rangers as a schoolboy in December 1968, having come from the youth side of home-town club Dundee United. He won himself a permanent place in fans' affections just one month later by scoring the only goal in the 1970-71 League Cup Final. Not only was this his first Cup Final – he was not even 17 at the time – it was also his first Old Firm match.

With such a dramatic start to his career, Johnstone always seemed destined for greatness. Not only did he establish himself in the Rangers squad of the 1970s which seemed to win titles at will, he was instrumental to their success. The sheer quantity of his honours was impressive enough, not to mention the fact that that he scored crucial goals in several

Finals and helped his side win trophies while playing in three positions – defence, midfield and centre-forward.

He collected medals for three League Championships, five League Cups, five Scottish Cups and the European Cup Winners' Cup of 1972. These honours included Rangers' Treble-winning years of 1976 and 1978.

As the club moved into the 1980s, Johnstone found himself faced with increasing pressures both with his performances on the pitch and his relationships with the management. He eventually left the club in 1983 and moved first to Chelsea and then on to his first love, Dundee United.

He stayed there for just one month before returning to Rangers in January 1985. He left a year later and currently reviews the Glasgow scene for Radio Clyde, secure in the knowledge that, while his return to Ibrox had been brief, no single player could compare with his entrance 16 years earlier in that first Old Firm match.

DEREK JOHNSTONE RANGERS RECORD 1970-83, 1985									
League		FA Cup		League Cup		Europe		Total	
Apps	Goals	Apps	Goals	Apps	Goals	Apps	Goals	Apps	Goals
369	132	57	30	85	39	35	9	546	210

 # DAVIE COOPER

Davie Cooper remains one of the modern heroes of Rangers folklore, his brilliance with the ball matched only by the inconsistency with which he produced those skills. When watching him you could never be sure if Davie would produce one of his dazzling runs to take him past an entire defence or simply give the ball to the opposition.

Whatever the result, it's certain that Cooper was one of the most gifted Scottish players of his or any other era. Born in

Hamilton on 25 February 1956, 'Coop' was known for his retiring nature. He originally played for Clydebank but moved to Rangers in June 1977, declaring himself 'the happiest guy in Scotland' after rejecting a number of offers from south of the border and accepting Jock Wallace's offer. Many mistook his quiet nature as a sign that he wasn't committed to Rangers, but he silenced his critics by letting his football do the talking.

In his first term at Ibrox, Rangers threw off an indifferent intervening season by winning the Treble for the second time in three years and continued the form established during the 1970s. Cooper's runs down the wing, his penetrating crosses to Gordon Smith and Derek Johnstone and the awesome power of his shot from set-pieces were crucial to this success and, increasingly, to the efforts of the national team. In addition to over 500 appearances at club level he also managed 22 caps (six goals) for Scotland.

His efforts for Rangers were rewarded by a healthy trophy cabinet which included three League Championships, three Scottish Cups and seven League Cups. Despite this success, to which Cooper was essential, he was transferred to Motherwell in August 1989. Far from being an end to his career, the move inspired Cooper, 33, to greater heights (notably a Cup win for the 'Well in 1991) which saw him returning to international duty after a lengthy absence. Returning to first club Clydebank in 1993 he continued to entertain. With his gifts, a career on the coaching side looked certain, but his death on 23 March 1995 as he coached youngsters at Clyde's Broadwood Stadium for a TV series, robbed both Glasgow and the game of a character.

DAVIE COOPER RANGERS RECORD 1977–89									
League		FA Cup		League Cup		Europe		Total	
Apps	Goals	Apps	Goals	Apps	Goals	Apps	Goals	Apps	Goals
377	49	49	7	74	18	35	1	535	75

ALLY MCCOIST

Whatever's said about 'Super' Ally McCoist, he can never be accused of shunning the limelight. Indeed, he positively hogs it. Always the extrovert, his antics both on and off the pitch are second only to his ability to score goals.

Born in Bellshill on 24 September 1962, McCoist did not at first feel the pull of Ibrox. Twice he rejected offers to join the club, favouring St Johnstone as a schoolboy and later Sunderland. It was at the third time of asking that he decided to move to Rangers after enjoying little success during two terms at Sunderland, and the deal was made in June 1983.

The pressure was immense in his first seasons at Ibrox, so much so that it was rumoured that the management were going to transfer him. But Ally battled against every obstacle in his path and after three years the fans gave him the respect his determination deserved. He responded with a feast of goals and international appearances, and feelings from the terraces soon developed from respect to reverence.

Aside from the League Championship medals which the present Rangers squad appear to have a standing order for, McCoist also has several League Cup medals and, up until Euro '96, was still a natural selection for the national team. He also holds several records including the highest ever scorer of League goals for Rangers (eclipsing the great Bob McPhail, whose record stood for fully 57 years) and the highest scorer in the history of the Scottish Premiership.

Super Ally has come a long way since he first donned the blue of Rangers and there are few players in the game today who celebrate scoring with the intensity that he shows. When he nets a goal his expression tells everyone he has scored for Rangers, his team. And the fans love him for it.

ALLY McCOIST RANGERS RECORD 1983-(97)									
League		FA Cup		League Cup		Europe		Total	
Apps	Goals	Apps	Goals	Apps	Goals	Apps	Goals	Apps	Goals
403	246	43	25	59	50	48	20	553	341

BRIAN LAUDRUP

Brian Laudrup's father, Finn, was capped 21 times for Denmark, while older brother Michael played for Barcelona and Juventus. Little wonder then that Laudrup, born in Vienna in February 1969, has proved one of the most naturally gifted players Scottish football has seen since arriving from Fiorentina in 1994.

Since beginning his career with Brondby, the globetrotting Laudrup has experienced football in Germany with Bayer Uerdingen and Bayern Munich (who paid £2 million to secure his services), as well as in Italy with Fiorentina and, on loan, AC Milan. Yet Walter Smith has allowed his speed and ball skills to be given full rein rather than force him to conform to a rigid system, with the result that the Dane was voted Player of the Year by sportswriters and players alike at the end of his first Rangers campaign, the 1994–95 season, after scoring 13 times in 38 matches.

Laudrup's unselfishness has given his fellow strikers McCoist and Durie many opportunities to prosper, while a total of 28 League goals in 88 League appearances to the start of the 1997–98 season was respectable enough for someone who naturally favours the wing rather than a central role.

BRIAN LAUDRUP RANGERS RECORD 1994-(97)									
League		FA Cup		League Cup		Europe		Total	
Apps	Goals	Apps	Goals	Apps	Goals	Apps	Goals	Apps	Goals
88	28	9	5	4	3	12	3	113	39

BEST SEASON 1

This was the first of two Double years in the early 1960s when League and Cup were captured – and though the following season saw the Treble of League, Cup and League Cup achieved, the 1962-63 campaign was hugely impressive in its own right.

It was the year the Big Freeze hit the British game, and, with the fixture congestion that ensued, it was indeed fortunate that Rangers had done the spadework for a nine-point margin at the top long before January 1963.

The classic half-back line of Greig, McKinnon and Baxter was in its pomp at this point, proving the engine room on which the side powered forward. The whole season saw only two games lost. The second, to runners-up Kilmarnock in May, was when it didn't really matter, and the superiority of the boys in blue was shown by the fact that the corresponding fixture at Ibrox had seen them run out conclusive 6-1 winners. (It would be Kilmarnock, however, that ended their interest in the League Cup at the semi-final stage, albeit thanks to a hotly disputed goal and by the slimmest of 3-2 margins.)

The FA Cup Final against Celtic will always be remembered as the match 'Slim' Jim Baxter, Rangers' midfield maestro, single-handedly avenged his club's 7-1 drubbing at the bands of Celtic in the League Cup Final of six years earlier. Some would say that had he not strutted, preened and even at one point allegedly sat on the ball then Rangers could well have emulated the scoreline instead of stopping at 3-0. It should in fairness be pointed out that this was a replay, the first game having finished goalless, but the win – thanks to goals from Brand (2) and Wilson – certainly put the gloss on the Double.

Rangers would go on to an equally impressive season in 1963-64, it being 14 matches before their League record was tainted by defeat. But injuries and age started doing their darndest to dismantle a very good team indeed. On the plus side, 1962-63 was the year young John Greig made his bid for a regular first-team place, grabbing the Number 4 shirt he'd wear with such distinction for the next decade and a half. The spearhead of Ralph Brand and Jimmy Millar scored 46 League goals between them, left-winger Davie Wilson chipping in with an amazing 23. At the back, custodian Billy Ritchie made sure no one scored more than two League goals in a game…little wonder this was a title–winning team!

1962-63 LEAGUE RECORD		
Opponents	Home	Away
Aberdeen	2-2	3-2
Airdrieonians	5-2	2-0
Celtic	4-0	1-0
Clyde	3-1	3-1
Dundee	1-1	0-0
Dundee United	5-0	1-2
Dunfermline A	1-1	2-1
Falkirk	4-0	2-0
Hearts	5-1	5-0
Hibernian	3-1	5-1
Kilmarnock	6-1	0-1
Motherwell	1-1	1-1
Partick Thistle	2-1	4-1
Queen of the South	3-1	4-0
Raith Rovers	4-2	2-2
St Mirren	3-0	2-0
Third Lanark	1-0	4-1

DERBY FOCUS

There are derbies, and there's the Glasgow derby. For all sorts of reasons – many, it must be said, nothing to do with football – the clash of the Glasgow giants has always been the prime fixture in Scottish, and indeed many would say British, footballing calendar.

The advent of the Scottish Premier League, reducing the élite and doubling the number of League clashes between the Glasgow giants (in addition to any possible Cup ties) may have multiplied the frequency, but it's arguable whether that's diluted any of the passion. Indeed, it's been in recent times that some of the most memorable derbies have been played. Where once a single goal would often prove decisive, the past decade has seen 3-3 and 4-4 added to the roll-call of scores registered over the years.

Further spice has been added by the addition of foreign players – specifically the Anglos imported in the late 1980s by Graeme Souness, when the fixture inherited the mantle of the Home International between Scotland and England, the oldest and most famous match between footballing nations which ended in 1989. More recently, Danes, Portuguese, Frenchmen, Germans and Serbs have played their part. All, however, understand the significance no matter what language they speak.

The Old Firm rivalry effectively began with the formation of Celtic Football and Athletic Club in 1888. Glasgow

Rangers had been established some 16 years previously. The rivals-to-be locked horns in Celtic's very first match and the home side ran out 5-2 winners.

The first Old Firm clash in the Scottish Cup took place in 1890, a mazy dribble and shot by Celtic's Willie Groves enough to take the honours. They first met in the Final itself in 1894, Rangers proving the winners by three goals to one, but five years on a similar win by Celtic deprived their rivals of a first League and Cup Double.

The boot would be on the other foot one decade later, as Celtic were seeking a hat-trick of 'Doubles' when they met Rangers in 1909. The first game ended in a 2-2 draw, the second 1-1 – but the Scottish FA withheld the Cup due to disgraceful scenes among supporters after 90 minutes.

The period between the wars saw Rangers amass 15 title wins to Celtic's five. But there was a sad reminder that football was only a game when the accidental clash of John Thomson and Sam English in a League fixture at Ibrox in September 1931 resulted in Celtic goalkeeper Thomson losing his life: players of both sides attended his funeral. Though Rangers forward English played on, he was never the same player and was transferred to Liverpool at the end of the 1932-33 season.

Derby games are supposed to be close-run affairs, but Rangers will be happy to forget the League Cup Final of October 1957, which Celtic won with embarrassing ease by 7-1. Though Rangers could point to wins like the 5-1 in September 1960 that got their Championship season off to a good start, another reverse against the old enemy, this time a 4-0 Scottish Cup Final in 1969, saw manager Davie White depart in favour of Willie Waddell. The new man presided over Rangers' 1970 League Cup victory by a single Derek Johnstone goal over the once-great Celtic side of the 1960s. This impetus continued when coach Jock Wallace was promoted to manager, the Centenary Cup Final in 1973 providing a memorable 3-2 victory.

RANGERS

Graeme Souness was the club's first player-manager, and his teams were as uncompromising as he was. But the Old Firm clash of 17 October 1987 went too far by ending not with the final whistle but in court. Woods, McAvennie and Butcher had all been dismissed for violent conduct, while Graham Roberts was also implicated. Woods and Butcher were found guilty in what was the first example of the Scottish legal system involving itself in matters on the pitch.

The 1987-88 campaign was disappointing for Rangers, Celtic taking seven points out of eight in the season's Old Firm derbies. But the balance was redressed in August 1988 with an impressive 5-1 victory in the opening Old Firm game of the new season. It would be the Gers' biggest League win of the season as they made their way to the first of an impressive string of League titles which would continue well into the 1990s, a decade where Rangers reigned supreme.

The New Year's Day clash in 1994 punctured Celtic's title pretensions as Rangers won 4-2. They went on to take their sixth successive League title, while Celtic faded, winning just five of their remaining 20 games. Gazza's Old Firm debut in November 1995 brought an entertaining 3-3 draw, the midfielder finding Ally McCoist's head with an artful free-kick to create his side's third goal.

The Scottish FA Cup Semi-Final of 7 April 1996, played at Hampden Park, saw Rangers push forward to the Double, overcoming a Celtic side on a roll of 29 games without defeat but with the Cup the only silverware they could realistically hope for. For 43 minutes all was quiet before Gordon Marshall's fumble was pounced upon by McCoist for his 16th Old Firm goal. Brian Laudrup played a neat one-two with Gordon Durie before lobbing the keeper from the edge of the box and, though Andy Goram was beaten in the 81st minute, a rampant Rangers had dashed Celtic's hopes once again.

The Old Firm became a worldwide phenomenon as names like Michael Laudrup, Paul Gascoigne, Marco Negri and

Jonas Thern were seen on the Ibrox team sheet. Celtic too imported some exotic names with skills to match, ensuring the Old Firm clash retained its status as the most newsworthy derby game of them all.

Historically, statistics suggest that Rangers have the edge in every single competition in which they've played their rivals, with the exception of Scottish FA Cup ties. In League terms, they're more or less 20 wins ahead, though League Cup honours are far less clear-cut. Nor should we forget the Glasgow Cup, a competition that for any other rivals would prove a footnote but which has thrown up some high-scoring games over the years.

The story so far

	P	W	D	L	F	A
League	244	97	73	74	359	318
FA Cup	40	13	8	19	52	62
League Cup	41	20	2	19	58	61
War Games etc	166	79	36	51	299	244
Total	**491**	**209**	**119**	**163**	**768**	**685**

RANGERS' TOP 10 DERBY APPEARANCES			
1	John Greig	1961-78	67
2	Sandy Jardine	1967-82	60
3	Derek Johnstone	1970-83, 1985	52
4	Ally McCoist	1983-(97)	47
5	Davie Cooper	1977-89	46
6	Peter McCloy	1970-85	45
7	Alex MacDonald	1968-80	44
8	Colin Jackson	1968-82	43
9	Ron McKinnon	1959-73	42
10=	Willie Johnston	1964-73, 1980-81	35
10=	Ian McColl	1947-59	35

THROUGH THE YEARS
MARCH

1876

March

25

Moses McNeil becomes the first of many Rangers players to represent Scotland when he faces Wales in Glasgow. The result was a 4-0 win for the home side.

1948

March

17

The birthdate of midfield terrier Alex McDonald, the tough-tackling Glaswegian who played over 300 games for Rangers after joining in 1968 from St Johnstone. He left in 1981 to become player-manager of Hearts, and later bossed Airdrie.

1995
March
23

Davie Cooper, Rangers' mercurial winger, dies age 39, having collapsed while supervising a kids training session for TV at Clyde's Broadwood Stadium. Hundreds lay scarves at Ibrox in a makeshift shrine to a much-loved player.

1996
March
16

Andy Dibble, a much-travelled English keeper, is plucked from the obscurity of Manchester City reserves to take the place of the injured Andy Goram – and the game, almost inevitably, is the last Old Firm clash of the season!

He managed to keep a clean sheet in the Parkhead inferno, while Brian Laudrup popped in the only goal of the game at the other end just on the half-time whistle to confirm the destination of the eighth Championship in a row. This of course equalled Celtic's record, set in the Jock Stein era.

Dibble would play out the season before giving way to another 'import', Bobby Gould's son Jonathan, signed from Bradford City.

FA CUP RECORD

Having competed in the Cup competition south of the border, Rangers have done well concentrating on the Scottish version. Here is their record.

Stage	Opponents	Score
1874-75		
Round 1	Oxford	2-0
Round 2	Dumbarton	0-0, 0-1
1875-76		
Round 1	First Lanark RV	7-0
Round 2	Third Lanark RV	*1-0, 1-2

* Third Lanark protested that Rangers kicked-off both halves

Stage	Opponents	Score
1876-77		
Round 1	Queen's Park J	4-1
Round 2	Towerhill	8-0
Round 3	Bye	
Round 4	Mauchline	3-0
Quarter-Final	Lennox	3-0
Semi-Final	Bye	
Final	Vale of Leven	1-1, 1-1, 2-3
1877-78		
Round 1	Possilpark	13-0
Round 2	Alexandra A	8-0
Round 3	Uddingston	13-0
Round 4	Vale of Leven	0-0, 0-5

Stage	Opponents	Score
1878-79		
Round 1	Shaftesbury	3-0
Round 2	Whitefield	6-1
Round 3	Parkgrove	8-2
Round 4	Alexandra A	3-0
Round 5	Partick	4-0
Quarter-Final	Queen's Park	1-0
Semi-Final	Bye	
Final	Vale of Leven	1-1
Rangers refused to replay the Final		
1879-1880		
Round 1	Queen's Park	0-0, 1-5
1880-81		
Round 1	Govan	4-1
Round 2	Northern	1-0
Round 3	Partick Thistle	3-0
Round 4	Clyde	11-0
Round 5	Hurlford	3-0
Quarter-Final	Dumbarton	1-3
1881-82		
Round 1	Third Lanark RV	2-1
Round 2	Harmonic	Walkover
Round 3	Alexandra A	3-1
Round 4	Thornliebank	2-0
Round 5	South Western	*2-1, 4-0
* Following a South Western protest the match was replayed		
Quarter-Final	Dumbarton	*1-2, 1-5
* Following a Rangers protest the match was replayed		
1882-83		
Round 1	Jordanhill	4-0
Round 2	Queen's Park	2-3

RANGERS

Stage	Opponents	Score
1883-84		
Round 1	Northern	1-0
Round 2	Whitehill	14-2
Round 3	Falkirk	5-2
Round 4	Dunblane	6-1
Round 5	St Bernards	3-0
Quarter-Final	Cambuslang	5-1
Semi-Final	Vale of Leven	0-3
1884-85		
Round 1	Whitehall	11-0
Round 2	Third Lanark RV	2-2, 0-0
	Both teams qualified	
Round 3	Third Lanark RV	3-0
Round 4	Arbroath	*3-4, 8-1
	Rangers protested about the size of the pitch	
Round 5	Bye	
Quarter-Final	Renton	3-5
1885-86		
Round 1	Clyde	0-1
1886-87		
Round 1	Govan A	9-1
Round 2	Westbourne	5-2
Round 3	Cambuslang	0-2
1887-88		
Round 1	Battlefield	4-1
Round 2	Partick Thistle	1-2
1888-89		
Round 1	Partick Thistle	4-2
Round 2	Clyde	2-2, 0-3

Stage	Opponents	Score
1889-90		
Round 1	United A	6-2
Round 2	Kelvinside A	13-0
Round 3	Vale of Leven	0-0, 2-3
1890-91		
Round 1	Celtic	0-1
1891-92		
Round 1	St Bernards	5-1
Round 2	Kilmarnock	0-0, 1-1, 3-2
Quarter-Final	Annbank	2-0
Semi-Final	Celtic	3-5
1892-93		
Round 1	Annbank	7-0
Round 2	Dumbarton	1-0
Quarter-Final	St Bernard	2-3
1893-94		
Round 1	Cowlairs	8-0
Round 2	Leith A	2-0
Quarter-Final	Clyde	5-0
Semi-Final	Queen's Park	1-1, 3-1
Final	Celtic	3-1
1894-95		
Round 1	Hearts	1-2
1895-96		
Round 1	Dumbarton	1-1, 3-1
Round 2	St Mirren	5-0
Quarter-Final	Hibernian	2-3

Stage	Opponents	Score
1896-97		
Round 1	Partick Thistle	4-2
Round 2	Hibernian	3-0
Quarter-Final	Dundee	4-0
Semi-Final	Morton	7-2
Final	Dumbarton	5-1
1897-98		
Round 1	Polton Vale	8-0
Round 2	Cartvale	12-0
Quarter-Final	Queen's Park	3-1
Semi-Final	Third Lanark RV	1-1, 2-2, 2-0
Final	Kilmarnock	2-0
1898-99		
Round 1	Hearts	4-1
Round 2	Ayr Parkhouse	4-1
Quarter-Final	Clyde	4-0
Semi-Final	St Mirren	2-1
Final	Celtic	0-2
1899-1900		
Round 1	Morton	4-2
Round 2	Maybole	12-0
Quarter-Final	Partick Thistle	6-1
Semi-Final	Celtic	2-2, 0-4
1900-01		
Round 1	Celtic	0-1
1901-02		
Round 1	Johnstone	6-1
Round 2	Caledonian	5-1
Quarter-Final	Kilmarnock	2-0
Semi-Final	Hibernian	0-2

Stage	Opponents	Score
1902-03		
Round 1	Auchterarder	7-0
Round 2	Kilmarnock	4-0
Quarter-Final	Celtic	3-0
Semi-Final	Stenhousemuir	4-1
Final	Hearts	1-1, 0-0, 2-0
1903-04		
Round 1	Hearts	3-2
Round 2	Hibernian	2-1
Quarter-Final	St Mirren	1-0
Semi-Final	Morton	3-0
Final	Celtic	2-3
1904-05		
Round 1	Ayr Parkhouse	2-1
Round 2	Morton	6-0
Quarter-Final	Beith	5-1
Semi-Final	Celtic	2-0
Final	Third Lanark	0-0, 1-3
1905-06		
Round 1	Arthurlie	7-1
Round 2	Aberdeen	3-2
Quarter-Final	Port Glasgow	0-1
1906-07		
Round 1	Falkirk	2-1
Round 2	Galston	4-0
Quarter-Final	Celtic	0-3
1907-08		
Round 1	Falkirk	2-2, 4-1
Round 2	Celtic	1-2

Stage	Opponents	Score
1908-09		
Round 1	St Johnstone	3-0
Round 2	Dundee	0-0, 1-0
Quarter-Final	Queen's Park	1-0
Semi-Final	Falkirk	1-0
Final	Celtic	2-2, 1-1

Following a riot at the replay, the competition was abandoned

1909-10		
Round 1	Inverness T	3-1
Round 2	Clyde	0-2

1910-11		
Round 1	Kilmarnock	2-1
Round 2	Morton	3-0
Quarter-Final	Dundee	1-2

1911-12		
Round 1	Stenhousemuir	3-1
Round 2	Clyde	1-3

Abandoned after 75 minutes

1912-13		
Round 1	Hamilton A	1-1, 2-0
Round 2	Falkirk	1-3

1913-14		
Round 1	Alloa A	5-0
Round 2	Hibernian	1-2

1919-20		
Round 1	Dumbarton	0-0, 1-0
Round 2	Arbroath	5-0
Round 3	Broxburn U	3-0
Quarter-Final	Celtic	1-0
Semi-Final	Albion Rovers	1-1, 0-0, 0-2

Stage	Opponents	Score
1920-21		
Round 2	Morton	2-0
Round 3	Alloa A	0-0, 4-1
Quarter-Final	Dumbarton	3-0
Semi-Final	Albion Rovers	4-1
Final	Partick Thistle	0-1
1921-22		
Round 1	Clachnacuddin	5-0
Round 2	Albion Rovers	1-1, 4-0
Round 3	Hearts	4-0
Quarter-Final	St Mirren	1-1, 2-0
Semi-Final	Partick Thistle	2-0
Final	Morton	0-1
1922-23		
Round 1	Clyde	4-0
Round 2	Ayr U	0-2
1923-24		
Round 1	Lochgelly U	4-1
Round 2	St Mirren	1-0
Round 3	Hibernian	1-2
1924-25		
Round 1	East Fife	3-1
Round 2	Montrose	2-0
Round 3	Arbroath	5-3
Quarter-Final	Kilmarnock	2-1
Semi-Final	Celtic	0-5
1925-26		
Round 1	Lochgelly U	3-0
Round 2	Stenhousemuir	1-0
Round 3	Falkirk	2-0
Quarter-Final	Morton	4-0
Semi-Final	St Mirren	0-1

RANGERS

Stage	Opponents	Score
1926-27		
Round 1	Leith A	4-1
Round 2	St Mirren	6-0
Round 3	Hamilton A	4-0
Quarter-Final	Falkirk	2-2, 0-1
1927-28		
Round 1	East Stirling	6-0
Round 2	Cowdenbeath	4-2
Round 3	King's Park	3-1
Quarter-Final	Albion Rovers	1-0
Semi-Final	Hibernian	3-0
Final	Celtic	4-0
1928-29		
Round 1	Edinburgh C	11-1
Round 2	Partick Thistle	5-1
Round 3	Clyde	2-0
Quarter-Final	Dundee U	3-1
Semi-Final	St Mirren	3-2
Final	Kilmarnock	0-2
1929-30		
Round 1	Queen's Park	1-0
Round 2	Cowdenbeath	2-2, 3-0
Round 3	Motherwell	5-2
Quarter-Final	Montrose	3-0
Semi-Final	Hearts	4-1
Final	Partick Thistle	0-0, 2-1
1930-31		
Round 1	Armadale T	7-1
Round 2	Dundee	1-2

Stage	Opponents	Score
1931-32		
Round 1	Brechin C	8-2
Round 2	Raith Rovers	5-0
Round 3	Hearts	1-0
Quarter-Final	Motherwell	2-0
Semi-Final	Hamilton A	5-2
Final	Kilmarnock	1-1, 3-0
1932-33		
Round 1	Arbroath	3-1
Round 2	Queen's Park	1-1, 1-1, 3-1
Round 3	Kilmarnock	0-1
1933-34		
Round 1	Blairgowrie	14-2
Round 2	Third Lanark	3-0
Round 3	Hearts	0-0, 2-1
Quarter-Final	Aberdeen	1-0
Semi-Final	St Johnstone	1-0
Final	St Mirren	5-0
1934-35		
Round 1	Cowdenbeath	3-1
Round 2	Third Lanark	2-0
Round 3	St Mirren	1-0
Quarter-Final	Motherwell	4-1
Semi-Final	Hearts	1-1, 2-0
Final	Hamilton A	2-1
1935-36		
Round 1	East Fife	3-1
Round 2	Albion Rovers	3-1
Round 3	St Mirren	2-1
Quarter-Final	Aberdeen	1-0
Semi-Final	Clyde	3-0
Final	Third Lanark	1-0

RANGERS

Stage	Opponents	Score
1936-37		
Round 1	Queen of the South	0-1
1937-38		
Round 1	Alloa A	6-1
Round 2	Queen of the South	3-1
Round 3	Bye	
Quarter-Final	Falkirk	2-1
Semi-Final	Kilmarnock	3-4
1938-39		
Round 1	Raith Rovers	1-0
Round 2	Hamilton A	2-0
Round 3	Clyde	1-4
1946-47		
Round 1	Clyde	2-1
Round 2	Hibernian	0-0, 0-2
1947-48		
Round 1	Stranraer	1-0
Round 2	Leith Athletic	4-0
Round 3	Partick Thistle	3-0
Quarter-Final	East Fife	1-0
Semi-Final	Hibernian	1-0
Final	Morton	1-1, 1-0
1948-49		
Round 1	Elgin C	6-1
Round 2	Motherwell	3-0
Round 3	Bye	
Quarter-Final	Partick Thistle	4-0
Semi-Final	East Fife	3-0
Final	Clyde	4-1

Stage	Opponents	Score
1949-50		
Round 1	Motherwell	4-2
Round 2	Cowdenbeath	8-0
Round 3	Bye	
Quarter-Final	Raith Rovers	1-1, 1-1, 2-0
Semi-Final	Queen of the South	1-1, 3-0
Final	East Fife	3-0
1950-51		
Round 1	Queen of the South	2-0
Round 2	Hibernian	2-3
1951-52		
Round 2	Elgin C	6-1
Round 3	Arbroath	2-0
Quarter-Final	Motherwell	1-1, 1-2
1952-53		
Round 1	Arbroath	4-0
Round 2	Dundee	2-0
Round 3	Morton	4-1
Quarter-Final	Celtic	2-0
Semi-Final	Hearts	2-1
Final	Aberdeen	1-1, 1-0
1953-54		
Round 1	Queen's Park	2-0
Round 2	Kilmarnock	2-2, 3-1
Round 3	Third Lanark	0-0, 4-4, 3-2
Quarter-Final	Berwick R	4-0
Semi-Final	Aberdeen	0-6
1954-55		
Round 5	Dundee	0-0, 1-0
Round 6	Aberdeen	1-2

Stage	Opponents	Score
1955-56		
Round 5	Aberdeen	2-1
Round 6	Dundee	1-0
Quarter-Final	Hearts	0-4
1956-57		
Round 5	Hearts	4-0
Round 6	Celtic	4-4, 0-2
1957-58		
Round 1	Cowdenbeath	3-1
Round 2	Forfar A	9-1
Round 3	Dunfermline A	2-1
Quarter-Final	Queen of the South	4-3
Semi-Final	Hibernian	2-2, 1-2
1958-59		
Round 1	Forfar A	3-1
Round 2	Hearts	3-2
Round 3	Celtic	1-2
1959-60		
Round 1	Berwick R	3-1
Round 2	Arbroath	2-0
Round 3	Stenhousemuir	3-0
Quarter-Final	Hibernian	3-2
Semi-Final	Celtic	1-1, 4-1
Final	Kilmarnock	2-0
1960-61		
Round 2	Dundee	5-1
Round 3	Motherwell	2-2, 2-5

Stage	Opponents	Score
	1961-62	
Round 1	Falkirk	2-1
Round 2	Arbroath	6-0
Round 3	Aberdeen	2-2, 5-1
Quarter-Final	Kilmarnock	4-2
Semi-Final	Motherwell	3-1
Final	St Mirren	2-0
	1962-63	
Round 2	Airdrieonians	6-0
Round 3	East Stirling	7-2
Quarter-Final	Dundee	1-1, 3-2
Semi-Final	Dundee U	5-2
Final	Celtic	1-1, 3-0
	1963-64	
Round 1	Stenhousemuir	5-1
Round 2	Duns	9-0
Round 3	Partick Thistle	3-0
Quarter-Final	Celtic	2-0
Semi-Final	Dunfermline A	1-0
Final	Dundee	3-1
	1964-65	
Round 1	Hamilton A	3-0
Round 2	Dundee U	2-0
Quarter-Final	Hibernian	1-2
	1965-66	
Round 1	Airdrieonians	5-1
Round 2	Ross County	2-0
Quarter-Final	St Johnstone	1-0
Semi-Final	Aberdeen	0-0, 2-1
Final	Celtic	0-0, 1-0
	1966-67	
Round 1	Berwick R	0-1

Stage	Opponents	Score
1967-68		
Round 1	Hamilton A	3-1
Round 2	Dundee	1-1, 4-1
Quarter-Final	Hearts	1-1, 0-1
1968-69		
Round 1	Hibernian	1-0
Round 2	Hearts	2-0
Quarter-Final	Airedrieonians	1-0
Semi-Final	Aberdeen	6-1
Final	Celtic	0-4
1969-70		
Round 1	Hibernian	3-1
Round 2	Forfar A	7-0
Quarter-Final	Celtic	1-3
1970-71		
Round 3	Falkirk	3-0
Round 4	St Mirren	3-1
Quarter-Final	Aberdeen	1-0
Semi-Final	Hibernian	0-0, 2-1
Final	Celtic	1-1, 1-2
1971-72		
Round 1	Falkirk	2-2, 2-0
Round 2	St Mirren	4-1
Quarter-Final	Motherwell	2-2, 4-2
Semi-Final	Hibernian	1-1, 0-2
1972-73		
Round 3	Dundee U	1-0
Round 4	Hibernian	1-1, 2-1
Quarter-Final	Airdrieonians	2-0
Semi-Final	Ayr U	2-0
Final	Celtic	3-2

Stage	Opponents	Score
1973-74		
Round 3	Queen's Park	8-0
Round 4	Dundee	0-3
1974-75		
Round 3	Aberdeen	1-1, 1-2
1975-76		
Round 3	East Fife	3-0
Round 4	Aberdeen	4-1
Quarter-Final	Queen of the South	5-0
Semi-Final	Motherwell	3-2
Final	Hearts	3-1
1976-77		
Round 3	Falkirk	3-1
Round 4	Elgin City	3-0
Quarter-Final	Motherwell	2-0
Semi-Final	Hearts	2-0
Final	Celtic	0-1
1977-78		
Round 3	Berwick R	4-2
Round 4	Stirling A	1-0
Quarter-Final	Kilmarnock	4-1
Semi-Final	Dundee U	2-0
Final	Aberdeen	2-1
1978-79		
Round 3	Motherwell	3-1
Round 4	Kilmarnock	1-1, 1-0
Quarter-Final	Dundee	6-3
Semi-Final	Partick Thistle	0-0, 1-0
Final	Hibernian	0-0, 0-0, 3-2

RANGERS

Stage	Opponents	Score
	1979-80	
Round 3	Clyde	2-2, 2-0
Round 4	Dundee U	1-0
Quarter-Final	Hearts	6-1
Semi-Final	Aberdeen	1-0
Final	Celtic	0-1
	1980-81	
Round 3	Airdrieonians	5-0
Round 4	St Johnstone	3-3, 3-1
Quarter-Final	Hibernian	3-1
Semi-Final	Morton	2-1
Final	Dundee U	0-0, 4-1
	1981-82	
Round 3	Albion R	6-2
Round 4	Dumbarton	4-0
Quarter-Final	Dundee	2-0
Semi-Final	Forfar A	0-0, 3-1
Final	Aberdeen	1-4
	1982-83	
Round 3	Falkirk	2-0
Round 4	Forfar A	2-1
Quarter-Final	Queen's Park	2-1
Semi-Final	St Mirren	1-1, 1-0
Final	Aberdeen	0-1
	1983-84	
Round 3	Dunfermline A	2-1
Round 4	Caledonian	6-0
Quarter-Final	Dundee	2-2, 2-3
	1984-85	
Round 3	Morton	3-3, 3-1
Round 4	Dundee	0-1

Stage	Opponents	Score
1985-86		
Round 3	Hearts	2-3
1986-87		
Round 3	Hamilton A	0-1
1987-88		
Round 3	Raith R	0-0, 4-1
Round 4	Dunfermline A	0-2
1988-89		
Round 3	Raith R	1-1, 3-0
Round 4	Stranraer	8-0
Quarter-Final	Dundee U	2-2, 1-0
Semi-Final	St Johnstone	0-0, 4-0
Final	Celtic	0-1
1989-90		
Round 3	St Johnstone	3-0
Round 4	Celtic	0-1
1990-91		
Round 3	Dunfermline A	2-0
Round 4	Cowdenbeath	5-0
Quarter-Final	Celtic	0-2
1991-92		
Round 3	Aberdeen	1-0
Round 4	Motherwell	2-1
Quarter-Final	St Johnstone	3-0
Semi-Final	Celtic	1-0
Final	Airdrieonians	2-1

Stage	Opponents	Score
1992-93		
Round 3	Motherwell	2-0
Round 4	Ayr U	2-0
Quarter-Final	Arbroath	3-0
Semi-Final	Hearts	2-1
Final	Aberdeen	2-1
1993-94		
Round 3	Dumbarton	4-1
round 4	Alloa Athletic	6-0
Quarter-Final	Hearts	2-0
Semi-Final	Kilmarnock	0-0, 2-1
Final	Dundee U	0-1
1994-95		
Round 3	Hamilton A	3-1
Round 4	Hearts	2-4
1995-96		
Round 3	Keith	10-1
Round 4	Clyde	4-1
Quarter-Final	Caledonian	3-0
Semi-Final	Celtic	2-1
Final	Hearts	5-1
1996-97		
Round 3	St Johnstone	2-0
Round 4	East Fife	3-0
Quarter-Final	Celtic	0-2

FA Cup Record Club By Club

Opposition	P	W	D	L	F-A
Aberdeen	23	14	4	5	39-28
Airdrieonians	6	6	—	—	21-2
Albion Rovers	9	5	3	1	20-8
Alexandra A	3	3	—	—	14-1
Alloa Athletic	5	4	1	—	21-2
Annbank	2	2	—	—	9-0
Arbroath	10	9	—	1	41-9
Armadale T	1	1	—	—	7-1
Arthurlie	1	1	—	—	7-1
Auchterarder	1	1	—	—	7-0
Ayr Parkhouse	2	2	—	—	6-2
Ayr U	3	2	—	1	4-2
Battlefield	1	1	—	—	4-1
Beith	1	1	—	—	5-1
Berwick R	4	3	—	1	11-4
Blairgowrie	1	1	—	—	14-2
Brechin C	1	1	—	—	8-2
Broxburn U	1	1	—	—	3-0
Caledonian	3	3	—	—	14-1
Cambuslang	2	1	—	1	5-3
Cartvale	1	1	—	—	12-0
Celtic	41	13	8	20	50-64
Clachnacuddin	1	1	—	—	5-0
Clyde	17	10	2	5	47-20
Cowdenbeath	7	6	1	—	28-6
Cowlairs	1	1	—	—	9-1
Dumbarton	14	7	3	4	25-15
Dunblane	2	1	—	1	7-3
Dundee	20	11	5	4	39-21
Dundee U	11	8	2	1	21-7
Dunfermline A	5	4	—	1	7-4
Duns	1	1	—	—	9-0
East Fife	7	7	—	—	19-2
East Stirling	2	2	—	—	13-2
Edinburgh C	1	1	—	—	11-1
Elgin C	3	3	—	—	15-2
Falkirk	16	11	3	2	35-17
First Lanark RV	1	1	—	—	7-0
Forfar A	6	5	1	—	24-4
Galston	1	1	—	—	4-0
Govan	2	2	—	—	13-2
Hamilton A	10	8	1	1	25-7
Hearts	28	18	5	5	61-29
Hibernian	27	11	7	9	38-33
Hurlford	1	1	—	—	3-0
Inverness T	1	1	—	—	3-1
Johnstone	1	1	—	—	6-1
Jordanhill	1	1	—	—	4-0
Keith	1	1	—	—	10-1
Kelvinside A	1	1	—	—	13-0
Kilmarnock	22	13	6	3	42-19
King's Park	1	1	—	—	3-1
Leith Athletic	3	3	—	—	10-1
Lennox	1	1	—	—	3-0
Lochgelly U	2	2	—	—	7-1
Mauchline	1	1	—	—	3-0
Maybole	1	1	—	—	12-0
Montrose	2	2	—	—	5-0
Morton	14	11	2	1	43-12
Motherwell	17	12	3	2	45-24
Northern	2	2	—	—	2-0
Oxford	1	1	—	—	2-0
Parkgrove	1	1	—	—	8-2
Partick Thistle	15	11	2	2	38-10
Polton Vale	1	1	—	—	8-0
Port Glasgow	1	—	—	1	0-1
Possilpark	1	1	—	—	13-0
Queen of the South	7	5	1	1	18-6
Queen's Park	15	9	4	2	30-15
Queen's Park J	1	1	—	—	4-1
Raith Rovers	9	5	4	—	18-4
Renton	1	—	—	1	3-5
Ross County	1	1	—	—	2-0
Shaftesbury	1	1	—	—	3-0
South Western	2	2	—	—	6-1
St Bernards	3	2	—	1	10-4
St Johnstone	10	8	2	—	23-4
St Mirren	17	14	2	1	40-9
Stenhousemuir	5	5	—	—	16-3
Stirling A	1	1	—	—	1-0
Stranraer	2	2	—	—	9-0
Third Lanark	17	8	7	2	28-17
Thornliebank	1	1	—	—	2-0
Towerhill	1	1	—	—	8-0
Uddingston	1	1	—	—	13-0
United A	1	1	—	—	6-2
Vale of Leven	9	—	5	4	7-17
Westbourne	1	1	—	—	5-2
Whitefield	1	1	—	—	6-1
Whitehall	1	1	—	—	11-0
Whitehill	1	1	—	—	14-2

CREAM OF THE CONTINENT

There's not a club in the Scottish or English top fight these days that doesn't have its fair share of exotic names. It's even been the source of a funny Kit-Kat ad, where *High Road* actor Ron Donachie does a passable Walter Smith impersonation as he tries to get his tactics over to a squad who clearly speak no English whatsoever!

Rangers have been one of the clubs leading the way in this regard, and it's easy to look back to Graeme Souness and his 'English invasion' that saw half the team consist of internationals who'd worn the three lions on their shirt. Chris Woods, Gary Stevens, Terry Butcher, Graham Roberts, Trevor Steven, Trevor Francis...and that's not counting the lesser lights like Drinkell, Woods, Rideout and Falco! The downside of this was that every match turned into a Scotland Versus England game, with all blue-blooded Scots eager to get one over on their (by now) blue-shirted opponents!

But you can look back further than that to catch Rangers' earliest foreigners. In 1965 the name of Danish-born Kai Johansen appeared in the right-back shirt, and he would prove a durable performer, missing four League games in the next three seasons. Sorenson and Persson kept the Scandinavian connection going, but there were few exotic names on the 1970s team-sheet (barring German custodian Gerry Neef) and it was only when John Greig signed Swede Robert Prytz, who filled a midfield role from 1982–85 and would actually line up against the Gers in European competition in the 1990s, that the Scots-Irish monopoly was broken.

Then came Souness, and every sports reporter north of the border was issued with an atlas as well as a *Rothmans*... Israeli keeper Bonnie Ginzburg understudied Chris Woods, while the name of Alexei Mikhailichenko was a challenge to fit on the back of even an extra-large shirt! Fellow Ukrainian Oleg Kuznetsov had other problems, a terrible leg injury sustained at St Johnstone in only his second game undoubtedly stopping Ibrox fans seeing the best of him.

Dutchman Pieter Huistra delighted – but erratically – during five seasons in which he clocked up nearly half as many subs appearances (38) as full (87). Ironically he left for Japan's J-League in 1995 as he hit his best ever form for the club, while Serbian defender Gordan Petric made the short move from Dundee United the same year after being introduced to Scottish football by countryman Ivan Golac.

Perhaps the foreigner whose face didn't fit in any way, shape or form was giant French stopper Basile Boli. A player his size was always going to stand out on the pitch, and his lack of mobility was apparent after his £2.7 million move from Marseille. If Smith made a bad buy there, then his acquisition of the current trinity of Laudrup, Gascoigne and Negri must be the best bit of shopping he's ever done. The great Dane was Player of the Year in his very first season, Gazza is still the mainstay of England's World Cup aspirations, while Negri's scoring record in the first half of the 1997–98 season was setting all records ablaze. Little wonder the great McCoist was packing his bags and heading south! Still on staff were Colombian Seb Rozental, who made just one League appearance as sub and dynamic Dane Erik Bo Anderson.

In the final analysis, Rangers players may come from different points of the compass, but it's their performance in the blue shirt that matters. Long may this continue...

THROUGH THE YEARS
APRIL

1877

April

Rangers played their first Scottish Cup Final today against Vale of Leven. The result was a 1-1 draw, but their opponents were awarded the trophy when Rangers refused to replay the match.

1961

April

29

Winger Alex Scott scores Rangers' 5,000th League goal against Ayr United at Ibrox. The scenario couldn't have been better: it's the last game of the season, Rangers are Champions, the score is 7-3 and Scott scored a hat-trick!

1986

April

6

After Jock Wallace's Rangers lose to Spurs 2-0 in a friendly in front of just 12,000 disinterested observers, Graeme Souness is called in to become Rangers' first ever player-manager.

1991

April

16

Souness packs his bags and heads back to Anfield, scene of his most glorious games as a player. The team he left won the title for the 40th time, and the third in successive seasons, but he found no comparable success at Liverpool.

1995

April

8

Neil Murray scores his very first League goal for Rangers after coming on as sub against Aberdeen when Basile Boli dislocates a shoulder. Rangers' 3–2 home win puts the Dons in evident danger of relegation (they escaped) but also clinches their seventh Championship, barring unlikely disasters.

20 THINGS YOU PROBABLY NEVER KNEW...

1 George Young, one of Rangers' greatest ever captains, was known as 'Corky' due to his habit of carrying a champagne cork on the pitch for good luck.

2 Walter Smith's playing career consisted of two spells at Dundee United, with 18 months at Dumbarton in-between. He was then assistant manager at Tannadice for four years before coming to Ibrox.

3 Future Manchester United manager Alex Ferguson signed from Dunfermline in 1967 and wore the Number 9 shirt with distinction, scoring 19 League goals in 29 games. He later had the chance to manage the club, but declined.

4 In January 1933 Ibrox played host to foreign opposition for the first time when mighty Rapid Vienna were the visitors for a friendly. The match ended in a 3-3 draw.

5 Rangers played a deciding match with Dumbarton to determine the destination of the first ever Scottish League title in 1891. The result was a 2-2 draw and the clubs were declared joint Champions.

6 When Erik Bo Andersen was signed from Danish club AaB Aalborg for £1.5 million in March 1996, his 24 goals for

Aalborg in 1994–95 was the highest total in domestic football for 14 years.

7 When Rangers' Danish full-back Kai Johansen chose to score his first goal since arriving in Scotland, he did so in the 1966 Cup Final replay against Celtic. It turned out to be the only goal of the game.

8 Rangers used to hold a sports day on the first Saturday in August, often attracting the world's top athletes. This was particularly popular between the wars due to the interest of ex-runner Bill Struth, then Rangers manager, but died out not long after his resignation in 1954.

9 Despite his perceived lack of success as a manager, playing legend John Greig brought McCoist, Fleck and Durrant to Ibrox and proved his dedication by returning in 1990 in a public relations capacity.

10 The 1994–95 season saw no fewer than 33 names appear on the Ibrox team sheet. Few clubs would have mounted a credible challenge in the face of such injuries, but a 15–game unbeaten run saw the Gers home for their seventh consecutive title.

11 Though banned from European competition after the pitch invasion that followed the Cup Winners' Cup win, Rangers played a Super Cup two-legger against European champions Ajax, losing on a 6–3 aggregate to the might of Cruyff, Rep and Krol.

12 Despite his many gifts, centre-half Willie Woodburn's poor disciplinary record earned him five sendings-off and an indefinite ban in 1954. Its lifting two and a half years later proved too late for him to make a comeback at age 38.

13 When Alan Morton, one of Rangers' greatest ever players, hung up his boots in 1932 he straightaway became a director of the club, and retained that status until his death in 1971. He is commemorated today by a painting in Ibrox's reception hall.

14 After the Stairway 13 tragedy in 1971, seven Rangers players took part in a benefit match in aid of the Disaster Fund. Five played in an Old Firm Select XI, bolstered by star guests from south of the border including Bonetti, Charlton and Best, while two more represented the opposition. The players were: Jardine, Greig, Smith, Henderson and Johnston (Old Firm Select) and McKinnon and Stein (Scotland XI).

15 Kenny Dalglish, best remembered in Scotland for his playing days at Celtic, was a huge Rangers fan and would have been delighted to have signed for the Ibrox club – but was sadly overlooked.

16 Legend has it that Rangers played their first game under the guise of 'Argyle': they changed their name when Moses McNeil, one of the youngsters who founded the club, saw the name in an English rugby annual!

17 Ralph Brand, who played over 300 games and scored 200 goals for Rangers between 1954 and 1965, was a lucky charm: playing in seven Cup Finals, he scored six goals and never once failed to pick up a winner's medal.

18 Captain John Greig made history in 1976 when he became Scottish Player of the Year for a second time – the only player ever to do the 'double'. Surprisingly, his first win had been exactly a decade earlier.

19 Rangers have played many times in Europe, but rarely been involved in a fracas as happened in Seville in 1962 when all 22 players on the pitch were reportedly involved in one altercation. Happily, a 4-0 first leg advantage saw the Gers through…albeit with a few bruises.

20 Rangers have always remembered former players, and when Scott Nisbet, forced to retire with a hip injury while still in his 20s, called it a day, a crowd of nearly 28,000 paid tribute at Ibrox as he was awarded a testimonial match in 1995.

FOR CLUB AND COUNTRY

As one of Scotland's leading clubs, you'll not be surprised to hear that Rangers have supplied many players to the Scottish national team. Yet as football north of the border has become more cosmopolitan, players from many other countries have lent support to the cause – and a significant number of international honours have been earned elsewhere.

The first Ranger to become a Scottish international was Moses McNeil, who donned the shirt with pride on 25 March 1876 when Scotland met Wales in Glasgow and ran out clear 4-0 winners. This honour was highly appropriate since he'd been one of the group of young men who'd formed the club back four years earlier – but since he'd then been just 16 years old, he would have qualified for an Under–21 team had one existed at that time.

Moving on to the postwar era, Iron Curtain defender George Young was for some years the record Scottish cap–holder, having gained 53 of them before retiring in 1957. An astounding 48 of them were as captain, a fact that paid tribute to his leadership qualities. A more recent Ibrox legend, Ally

McCoist, was made Scotland captain for his 50th international against Australia, and by the start of 1997–98 had reached a record 58 caps. Ironically, he was about to leave Ibrox in a search for a first-team place elsewhere that would give him the chance of a World Cup swansong in France '98. Scotland's finest hour against England had surely come in 1928, when the Wembley Wizards whipped England 5-1 on home turf in 1928. Alan Morton, who picked up his 'Wee Blue Devil' nickname in that fame, was the only Rangers player in the team – and was ever-present in the annual fixture from 1921 to 1932. The exception was 1926 when, significantly, England won 1-0 in Manchester.

Yet when it comes to club versus country, the ultimate test surely came 70 years later in 1996 when Paul Gascoigne faced team-mate Andy Goram in the European Championships for England against Scotland. Showing no mercy, the gifted midfielder swept the ball past his club keeper to register his country's second goal, putting glory beyond Craig Brown's troops for another campaign. Goram's alleged post-match remarks are perhaps best left unrepeated…

WORST SEASON 1

Few seasons that begin with three wins on the bounce end up as disappointingly as did 1925-26. One of the reasons for Rangers' slump to sixth place, still the club's record low in the top flight of Scottish football, was a spate of bad injuries.

No fewer than seven internationals – Archibald, Cairns, Cunningham, McCandless, Meiklejohn, Morton and Muirhead – were ruled out for substantial spells, leaving a threadbare side that proved unable to retain the Championship trophy that had resided in the Ibrox boardroom for the past three seasons.

A disastrous December brought only three points, after which it was clear that the Cup offered the only real chance of salvaging any pride from the season. The omens looked good, but after rolling over Lochgelly, Stenhousemuir, Falkirk and Morton to reach the Semi-Final, St Mirren scored the only goal of a dour match at Parkhead to leave Rangers down and out.

And down they most certainly were: sixth place was only achieved after a remarkable winning streak in April when they won three games out of four and drew the other to end sixth with 44 points and avoid a lower-half finish which would surely have been beyond forgiveness. Even so, Celtic (who topped the League) finished 14 points ahead of their neighbours and rivals, while fully 13 of the season's 38 fixtures had been lost...both miserable statistics the Ibrox faithful found hard to digest.

Many of the players who appeared in this season's team would soon find themselves replaced: Dixon, Craig and J Hamilton of the defence who totalled 97 League appearances between them, amassed but a handful in 1926–27, while centre-forward Henderson was replaced by the freer-scoring Marshall.

Needless to say, the position of long-serving Bill Struth, in charge since 1920, was not a subject for debate, and indeed he would guide his charges back to the top in 1926–27 – a position they would happily retain for five seasons. This, then was a blip, not a disaster.

1925-26 LEAGUE RECORD		
Opponents	**Home**	**Away**
Aberdeen	0-1	1-3
Airdrieonians	1-2	1-2
Celtic	1-0	2-2
Clydebank	3-1	2-2
Cowdenbeath	3-0	3-2
Dundee	1-2	5-1
Dundee United	2-1	1-2
Falkirk	2-3	1-1
Hamilton A	2-0	3-3
Hearts	2-2	0-3
Hibernian	3-1	2-0
Kilmarnock	3-0	2-2
Morton	4-1	3-1
Motherwell	1-0	3-1
Partick Thistle	2-1	0-2
Queen's Park	1-2	6-3
Raith Rovers	4-2	0-1
St Johnstone	0-1	3-0
St Mirren	4-1	2-3

DOUBLE ACTS

Mark Hateley and Ally McCoist developed an enviable understanding over the five seasons they played together. It was the smaller, more mobile Scot who picked up the records and plaudits, but he would be the first to admit he owed much to the knockdowns, hustling and general leadership of the tall Englishman.

Initially Hateley, signed from Monaco and son of 1960s Liverpool striker Tony, stepped into McCoist's shoes alongside Mo Johnston and all three, plus Mark Walters, got into double figures. But McCoist got up off the bench to register 34 League goals to Hateley's 21 in the next season (over half the club's total between them), then 34 (19) before injuries intervened. Hateley's value to Rangers and McCoist in particular was underlined when Walter Smith brought him back to Ibrox in 1997 after spells with QPR and Leeds, but McCoist too was at the end of his reign and the spark between them could not be rekindled. Nevertheless, it was a classic Little and Large-style act while it lasted.

Known as the 'Wee Blue Devil' (a description given by an English spectator at the Wembley drubbing of England in 1928), diminutive outside-left Alan Morton formed two great partnerships at Ibrox. The first with inside-left Tommy Cairns stretched through to 1927, whereupon Bob McPhail took over the Number 10 shirt to form an equally deadly partnership. Morton was adept at cutting in and scoring himself when not setting up chances for his partner, and nine

Championship medals resulted. His record of nearly 500 games for Rangers tells part of the story, and certainly Cairns, McPhail and Scotland team-mate Alec Jackson of Huddersfield had cause to enjoy the double act he set up with all three for club and country. Morton was the epitome of a team player.

Jim Baxter's skills could fill a book on their own. Yet any creative midfield player who plied his trade before today's 'track-back' orders needed an industrious, defensive-minded partner to fall back and plug the gap that inevitably occurred when the playmaker sniffed an opportunity.

Yet Rangers somehow managed with two free spirits, for Ian McMillan was as carefree a performer as Baxter himself. He was a surveyor by trade and played football on a strictly part-time basis, something else that would not be permitted today – but his down to earth personality ensured he avoided the problems his big-name partner encountered. Though both players needed a defensive double act of Harold Davis and Eric Caldow to cover their shortcomings, they gave the Ibrox crowds plenty to smile about with some spirited play.

Full-backs Jock Drummond and Nicol Smith proved the backbone of a great defence in Rangers' first great team. League and Cup honours were thick on the ground as the cloth-capped Drummond, signed from Falkirk, and Ayr-born Smith (dubbed the Darvel Marvel after his birthplace) kept all-comers at bay.

The partnership was cemented in 1893-94 and continued unabated until 1902, yet another Championship year, with keeper Dickie a superb third party since 1896. Sadly, Smith, whose career was blighted by injury, died of enteric fever at the tragically early age of 32, shortly after his wife, and a testimonial was played for their children. Drummond returned to Falkirk where he'd later coach and become a director.

Richard Gough's arrival at Ibrox by a roundabout route from Dundee United paired him with the player Spurs had originally sought when they signed him – ex-Ipswich and England stopper Terry Butcher. Together they formed an impregnable central defensive barrier which was the basis on which the first two consecutive Championships was founded. Indeed with fellow international Chris Woods behind them and stalwart full-backs Stevens and Munro, this was the nearest equivalent of the famed Iron Curtain defence old-time Rangers fans had seen. Butcher was on his way south and Dave McPherson had to be recalled to replace him. Impressive results continued, but the impregnability had gone.

John Greig and Ron McKinnon bolstered the heart of Rangers' 1960s defence after the former was moved back from old-fashioned inside-forward to play sweeper alongside McKinnon's stopper.

Unfortunately injury stopped McKinnon from sharing in his colleague's joy as he raised the Cup Winners' Cup in 1972, but for most of the preceding decade they had presented an impressive barrier as Rangers finished a consistent second in the League to Jock Stein's Celtic. In international terms too Greig eclipsed his team-mate, but would be the first to admit that their skills complemented each other perfectly whether in League action or in the darker blue of Scotland, which Greig also captained.

This notably incisive forward pairing both made their Rangers debuts in the reserves as schoolboys in the same match in 1936, and on graduating would carry their relationship into the first team with no little success. Both players were exemplary in their conduct: Waddell later became manager, while Thornton, who was often the recipient of his team-mate's pinpoint crosses, was never booked. It was largely his goals that gave Rangers first place in four out of five postwar seasons, with outside-right Waddell the chief provider.

The Iron Curtain defence that brought Rangers such success between 1946 and 1953 was founded on players who remained free from injury and suspension. In 1949–50, they conceded just six goals in 30 games and full–backs Young and Shaw missed just one game between them.

Six foot two inches and 15 stone George Young had moved to Number 2 from central defence to accommodate Willie Woodburn, while Jock Shaw won the nickname 'Tiger' due to his uncompromising tackling. At the end of the 1949–50 season referred to he was 38, but played on for four more years before becoming Rangers trainer. Young went on till 1957, captaining Scotland 48 times. Both players earned their place in legend.

THROUGH THE YEARS
MAY

1872
May

Rangers' first recorded game on Glasgow Green against Callendar ends in a 0-0 draw. Another fixture later in the month sees Clyde demolished 11-0.

1941
May
31

Legendary England winger Stanley Matthews makes a guest appearance for Rangers in the Glasgow Charity Cup Final against Partick. Rangers win 3-0 with goals by Gillick (2) and Venters.

1965
May
25

The end of an era as midfield genius Jim Baxter leaves Ibrox for Sunderland. He would never recapture the form that made him a Rangers idol at Sunderland and Nottingham Forest, though he returned to the club briefly in 1969-70 to make 14 more appearances.

1972
May
24

Rangers' finest hour in Europe as a 3-2 win over Moscow Dynamo gave them their first ever continental trophy. Having established a 3-0 lead, they took their foot off the gas, allowing the Russians to make a game of it.

1979
May
28

New manager John Greig wins his first trophy since his playing days – the Scottish FA Cup. But what an effort! Two games against Hibernian both finishing goalless, the third ends 3-2 and, despite two goals from the dependable Derek Johnstone, is settled only after Hibs' Duncan puts the ball past his own goalkeeper.

1996
May
18

The most recent of Rangers' 27 Scottish Cup wins is achieved with no little style in a 5-1 demolition of Hearts at Hampden. Durie (3) and Laudrup (2) share the spoils and complete the Double.

GREAT MIDFIELDERS

The Ibrox success story has always featured playmakers and ball-winners. Here are five of the very best midfield operators in Rangers' long and glorious history.

 ## JIM BAXTER

Three full decades have passed since his heyday, yet James Curran Baxter remains the most revered midfielder ever to wear the blue shirt of Rangers. Manager Scot Symon signed Baxter from Raith Rovers in June 1960 for a record fee of £17,500. That outlay was repaid as Rangers took 10 of the 15 domestic trophies for which they competed during Bazter's five years at Ibrox – three League Championship medals, three Scottish Cups and four League Cups.

In 1963, Baxter bagged both goals as a ten-man Scotland outfit beat Alf Ramsey's men 2-1 at Wembley. In the same year, his talent was given a larger stage as he represented a European XI against England in the Football Association Centenary match, again at Wembley.

Baxter signed for Sunderland in May 1965 for a fee of £72,500, moving on to Nottingham Forest for £100,000 two years later, but was never to fulfil his potential south of the border. His return to Ibrox for a season was unimpressive and his decline, due to an over-fondness for alcohol, was as rapid as it was sad and he was lost to the game he graced so magnificently.

JIM BAXTER RANGERS RECORD 1960-65									
League		FA Cup		League Cup		Europe		Total	
Apps	Goals	Apps	Goals	Apps	Goals	Apps	Goals	Apps	Goals
136	18	21	—	50	2	25	2	232	22

JOHN GREIG

John Greig epitomises the Rangers tradition of strong, hard-working players who make up what they lack in delicate skills with their conviction to the cause. This is by no means a criticism. Many view Greig as one of the best players ever to don the Rangers colours and his performances over two decades more than back up this claim.

Born in Edinburgh on 11 September 1942, John made his first-team debut against Airdrie in the League Cup in September 1961. He got off to a promising start by scoring and this led to him often taking on an attacking role, although his favoured position was central defence. This enabled him to impose his presence on the game, allowing him to watch over his team and also providing a daunting barrier for any would-be scorer.

Greig was a natural leader and captained his side by example, fighting to the end no matter what the odds. He led both club and country but enjoyed greater success with Rangers, averaging almost a trophy a season during his 17 campaigns with the club as a player. Greig continued his leadership after he retired from the game, totalling over 750 appearances for Rangers, and took over the club as manager in May 1978.

His playing record is without equal, having amassed five Championship medals, six Scottish Cup medals and four League Cup medals. These honours include a staggering three Treble seasons (1963-64, 1975-76 and 1977-78) when Rangers won the major domestic titles. Greig also enjoyed success on a larger stage when Rangers took the European Cup Winners' Cup in 1972 by beating Moscow Dynamo 3-2 in Barcelona. This impressive career also includes 44 appearances for Scotland and an MBE for his services to football.

JOHN GREIG RANGERS RECORD 1960-78									
League		FA Cup		League Cup		Europe		Total	
Apps	Goals	Apps	Goals	Apps	Goals	Apps	Goals	Apps	Goals
498	87	72	9	121	17	64	7	755	120

 # ALEX MacDONALD

Like so many of Rangers' greatest players, Alex 'Doddie' MacDonald was a key player in the squad which dominated Scottish football during the 1970s. He displayed great tackling ability and endurance, and became the workhorse of the midfield who was given the extra responsibility of winning the ball from the opposition to set up his more creative colleagues.

A local lad, Alex was born on 17 March 1948 and began his professional career by playing for St Johnstone. He moved to Rangers in November 1968 but met initial opposition from supporters and took some time to settle into the squad. He eventually overcame his problems and his competitiveness finally endeared him the fans, so much so that he became one of their favourites.

As well as his reputation as a ball-winner, Doddie was also known for scoring goals at critical moments. Of these few can have been as important, or as sweet, as his winning goal over Celtic in the League Cup Final in 1976 which allowed Rangers to go on and complete the Treble of Championship, League Cup and Scottish Cup.

Alex was again part of the Treble squad in 1977-78 and these two seasons contributed greatly towards his honours at the club. These included three League Championships, four Scottish Cups and four League Cups as well as the European Cup Winners' Cup in 1972.

After 12 years of service MacDonald moved to Hearts in 1980 where he played a season before becoming player-manager. He then went on to manage the club full-time, showing the same determination that he played with, which culminated in the Manager of the Year award in 1986. After leaving Tynecastle, he became manager of Airdrie, leading them to the Scottish Cup Final in 1995.

ALEX MacDONALD RANGERS RECORD 1968-80									
League		FA Cup		League Cup		Europe		Total	
Apps	Goals	Apps	Goals	Apps	Goals	Apps	Goals	Apps	Goals
336	51	50	15	79	18	38	10	503	94

 # STUART McCALL

Midfield dynamo Stuart McCall was transferred to Rangers in August 1991 from Everton after beginning his career with Bradford City, where both England and Scotland selected him to play in their Under-21 teams on the same day. He'd recently scored two goals in 1989's all-Merseyside FA Cup Final after coming off the substitutes' bench – a history-making feat equalled by Liverpool's Ian Rush, who emerged on the winning side that day.

After choosing to play his international football for the country of his father's birth, rather than that of his own, McCall has gathered 39 full Scottish caps (to the beginning of 1997-98). The move to Ibrox didn't hinder his cause, and he played in all three of Scotland's games in the Finals of Euro '96. McCall has proved the ideal midfield foil to Paul Gascoigne, just as he wins the ball for Gary McAllister in Scotland's darker blue.

Now well into his early thirties, Stuart McCall is not only one of Rangers' elder statesmen but an increasing rarity – a Scot. Unfortunately, the 1996-97 season saw him sidelined by a succession of injuries, becoming a treatment-table regular after the first seven League games and a handful of Cup ties. He was ready, willing and able to play a greater part in his seventh season at Ibrox as Rangers went for 'ten in a row'.

STUART McCALL RANGERS RECORD 1991-(97)									
League		FA Cup		League Cup		Europe		Total	
Apps	Goals	Apps	Goals	Apps	Goals	Apps	Goals	Apps	Goals
164	15	20	—	15	3	26	2	225	20

 # PAUL GASCOIGNE

When Paul Gascoigne turned down a return to English football in late 1997, the blue half of Glasgow let out a sigh of relief. It was proof that the clown prince of soccer had carved a place for himself in Rangers folklore, proving in two years at Ibrox that, despite the doubters, he still had what it took.

RANGERS

Walter Smith paid Lazio £4.5 million to bring the one-time Newcastle United and Tottenham midfielder to Ibrox, primarily in a bid to improve Rangers' European fortunes. Gazza's playmaking ability continued to be evident in flashes, while goals proved the icing on the cake: he registered a hat-trick against Motherwell in October 1996, following a truly memorable goal in the 1996 European Championships against Scotland and club colleague Andy Goram.

He's averaged a goal every two games since his September 1995 introduction against Raith Rovers. On the down side, a sending-off in the November 1997 Old Firm game after tussling with Celtic's Wieghorst, which led to a lengthy suspension, suggested he was still on a knife-edge temperamentally, and his domestic arrangements remained front-page news.

His contribution to Rangers' League and Cup Double in 1996-97 was undoubted, however, and he was voted Scotland's Player of the Year against some stiff competition. And, as England qualified for the 1998 World Cup, he completed a half-century of international caps, proving as crucial to Glenn Hoddle's plans as to Terry Venables before him.

Walter Smith has retained faith in Gascoigne, a man whose close control and ability to take on defenders make him a real force in club football. He clearly didn't want him to leave, and was pleased to retain his man in the face of Aston Villa's interest. Gazza belonged to Glasgow – and all parties were delighted.

PAUL GASCOIGNE RANGERS RECORD 1995-(97)

League		FA Cup		League Cup		Europe		Total	
Apps	Goals	Apps	Goals	Apps	Goals	Apps	Goals	Apps	Goals
54	27	5	3	7	4	10	2	76	36

PLAYER TALK

Footballers have brains in their boots – but these Ibrox favourites chose to put their thoughts into words

'I'm right at home here, and it's a tremendous honour to be the first foreigner to win the award.'

Brian Laudrup on winning Scottish
Football Writers' Player of the Year

'We're going through a period which will be remembered for a long time by Rangers fans, and that's why I really want to achieve ten in a row. I'm confident that I have that left in me.'

Richard Gough

'The game in Scotland is much faster than English football. Consequently it is much more physical…players want to square up to you all the time.'

Terry Butcher

'For a while I did unite Rangers and Celtic fans. There were people in both camps who hated me.'

Maurice Johnston

'I just want to get on with enjoying my football again, and I know I'll do that at Rangers.'

Paul Gascoigne

'The Italian press say I went to Rangers only for the money, but that's not true. I owe Rangers a lot. They came in for me after only one season in *Serie A* – it's not as if I was Maradona.'

Marco Negri

'The boy Rudyard Kipling, who said it wasn't whether you won but how you play the game that mattered, obviously never played football. Winning is the only thing that matters.'
Andy Goram

'Gazza is one of the biggest talents the English game has ever produced...'
Brian Laudrup

'Paul Gascoigne's an intelligent boy who likes to let people think he's stupid.'
Ally McCoist

'We have players who actually prefer playing away because of the nature of the Rangers support. I prefer our away following – they get behind the team far better.'
Richard Gough

'I hope to be here so long they have to kick me out!'
Andy Goram

'A lot of players do a lot of things outside football. But another player doesn't have a photographer stuck up his backside.'
Paul Gascoigne

'We should be looking to win every game by 4-0 or 5-0 because we have better players.'
Richard Gough

'The only advice I ever had about money was from turf accountants.'
Jim Baxter

'We call Ally McCoist Golden Bollocks. He's Superman and Roy of the Rovers rolled into one.'
Scotland team-mate John Robertson

'The amount of running I do means I'm not going to play in midfield forever.'
Stuart McCall

THROUGH THE YEARS
JUNE

1947
June
2

Winger Tommy McLean is born at Ashgill. He registered over 450 games in all competitions after arriving from Kilmarnock in 1971, repaying his £65,000 fee many times over, and later became assistant manager to John Greig.

1964
June
10

Stuart McCall is born in Leeds, his Scottish father assuring him of the right to represent two countries. Ironically, England and Scotland Under-21s called him up on the very same day! The flame-haired midfielder chose to play his club football north of the border too, joining Rangers from Everton in 1991.

1968
June
4

An end-of-season Scandinavian tour closes with an emphatic 5-1 win against Gothenburg. Appropriately, Orjan Persson weighs in with two of the goals in a result that confirms a four win out of four record, Frem (4-1), Odense (2-0) and Sydjysk (3-1) having been previously vanquished.

1984
June
2

Rangers take on the Australian national side in Sydney, having already drawn with and beaten the B team during the World Soccer Series tournament. Despite two goals from Ally McCoist, Rangers lose 3-2, though a further game against Australia B is drawn to leave them with an even record in the four games.

1991
June

Rangers this month paid their record fee, £2.5 million, for the services of Alexei Mikhailichenko from Italian club Sampdoria. Two months later, they were to record their record fee obtained for a player, selling midfielder Trevor Steven to Marseille for a cool £5,580,000 – and, unlike 'Miko's price tag, that haul remains in the history books.

GREAT MATCHES

**A club like Glasgow Rangers has played
many memorable matches over the years.
We've picked five of the very best from the
post-war era to give a taste of this rich and
varied history, ranging from friendlies to
Cup Finals and beyond.**

Rangers 2 Moscow Dynamo 2
28 November 1945
Friendly

Rangers' record in Europe, though somewhat short on silverware, has been almost continuous since club competitions started in the mid 1950s. Their very first brush with European competition however came a decade earlier – just after the end of the war in November 1945.

Ironically the opposition was the same as when they would win the Cup Winners Cup in 1972, but in this case Moscow Dynamo were playing a tour that included visits to Chelsea, Arsenal and Cardiff. They'd played all the other three – complaining about the number of guest players Arsenal had fielded – and remained unbeaten as they arrived at Ibrox to battle it out against 11 men and 95,000 expectant fans.

The visitors quickly silenced the 95,000 with two well-taken goals in the first half-hour, and worse was to come when the normally dependable Willie Waddell had a spot-kick tipped over the bar. There was confusion among the substitutes (allowed in this friendly game) as the Muscovites at one point fielded 12 men in error, but despite their brief numerical inferiority Rangers fought back. Jimmy Smith equalised, and when a second, disputed penalty was awarded in the final minutes up stepped brawny George Young to do the honours. A draw saw honour satisfied.

The game would prove the swansong of long-serving goalkeeper Jerry Dawson, while several famous names, including spearhead Smith, would be missing come the following season.

Team: Dawson, David Gray, Shaw, Watkins, Young, Symon, Waddell, Gillick, Smith, Williamson, Johnstone.

> ## Celtic 1 Rangers 5
> ## 10 September 1960
> ## League Division One

With an hour gone, there was no indication that this, the fourth Old Firm derby in as many weeks, would be anything other than another keenly-fought contest with, perhaps, a modest margin of victory to this side or that. True, Rangers had opened the scoring after just two minutes, Scott pouncing on John Fallon's poorly-punched clearance to leave the Celtic keeper without a hope, but the game was evenly balanced throughout the remainder of the first half, and looked like staying that way until Rangers scored their second in the 66th minute.

Kurila, who had policed Millar very successfully until this time, was unfortunate when he tackled Wilson and could only watch as the ball rebounded conveniently to the Rangers centre-forward. Millar took the ball forward, rounded McKay and was lucky to get another chance when his initial shot was parried by Fallon. He made no mistake the second time, and Rangers were two up.

Now playing with the confidence given by that two-goal cushion, Rangers shifted up a gear and Celtic began to look outclassed. Three further goals in seven minutes underlined the difference between the sides towards the end of the game. First, Brand capitalised on Fallon's failure to gather Millar's 78th-minute cross, and then, six minutes later, Brand was again involved as he put Wilson through for Rangers' fourth. Finally, Davis, the best player on either side, completed the humiliation by turning in Scott's 85th-minute corner kick, and Rangers became the first side to put five past Celtic in a League fixture at Parkhead since Aberdeen in January 1947.

The home side gained a last-minute consolation goal through young Stevie Chalmers. In fairness to Celtic, theirs was not a performance to be ashamed of. Rather, this was a game won by a side which found irresistible form late on and which would go on to win a further 22 games in a Championship-winning campaign.

Team: Ritchie, Shearer, Caldow, Davis, Paterson, Baxter, Scott, McMillan, Millar, Brand, Wilson.

Rangers 3 Moscow Dynamo 2
24 May 1972
European Cup Winners' Cup Final

Rangers had made it to the Cup Winners' Cup Final twice before, losing to Fiorentina (1961) and Bayern Munich (1967) – and it was to prove third time lucky when, facing Moscow Dynamo in Barcelona, they swept into a seemingly unassailable 3-0 lead in front of a crowd made up almost exclusively of Glaswegians. Up until the hour mark it was a dream game, Colin Stein having thundered home from the edge of the area on 24 minutes and Willie Johnston scored with a rare header some 15 minutes later. Both goals were made by the penetrating passes of Dave Smith, an unsung hero on a night of pure passion.

Johnston appeared to make the game safe with Rangers' third, just four minutes after the restart, and it only seemed a question of how many the hapless Russian team would concede. But as their fans' booze-fuelled bravado subsided, Rangers took their foot off the gas. The Russians made a tactical substitution and the new man, Eshtrekov, used his fresh legs to power forward and reduce the arrears. The game entered a new phase as Dynamo sensed a chance. Thankfully, their second goal, through Mekoikov, came with just three minutes left. Rangers thankfully held out for a win that looked far more slender on paper than it had needed to be.

The night nevertheless goes down as one of Rangers' all-time highlights as it remains the first piece of European silverware they have yet to claim. Unfortunately, security at the mighty Nou Camp Stadium was non-existent, and the exuberance of certain fans combined with the release of tension meant that crowd trouble would bar the club from defending their prize the following season.

On the other hand, they could look back on a campaign that had seen them vanquish Torino and Bayern Munich – and nearly go out against Sporting Lisbon when a confused referee ordered the match, tied at 6-6, to be decided by penalties. Thankfully the UEFA observer was on hand to tell him that away goals counted double and that the Portuguese had not won after all. On such things are Cups won and lost!

Team: McCloy, Jardine, Mathieson, Greig, Johnstone, Smith, McLean, Conn, Stein, A MacDonald, Johnston.

> **Rangers 3 Celtic 2**
> **5 May 1973**
> **Scottish FA Cup Final**

Old Firm games are all about pride and tradition, history and emotion, but few can have rivalled the Centenary Scottish FA Cup Final on any of these counts. Rangers had endured seven long years of disappointment and frustration, the only relief being provided by their League Cup victory two seasons earlier and the previous year's Cup Winners' Cup win.

But even their European success had been tainted by crowd disturbances after the Final, and what became known as the 'Battle of Barcelona' led to a ban from European competition which deprived them of the opportunity of defending the trophy.

In addition, this was Rangers' own Centenary year and, with Celtic League Champions for the eighth successive season and the League Cup safely in the trophy cabinet at Easter Road, this was the last chance the club would have to mark this important occasion.

Rangers went into the match unbeaten in 25 games since December, an impressive run which had seen them to within a whisker of taking the League Championship, but Celtic had held off the challenge and remained hot favourites for the Double. It turned out to be a wet day, but as the teams took to the field in front of a crowd of over 120,000, the grey skies and steady rain had no chance of dampening the spirit of the occasion.

The match got off to much the expected start. Celtic were marginally the better side in the opening period, and took a 25th-minute lead when Deans' through ball found Dalglish who skilfully slipped the ball past the advancing McCloy. Rangers redoubled their efforts, and equalised ten minutes later when Alec MacDonald's cross found Derek Parlane's head and the ball beat Hunter on his right side.

The second half opened in spectacular fashion. Within 20 seconds of the kick-off, Alfie Conn had shown Billy McNeill a clean pair of heels – and, although Hunter did his best to narrow the angle, Conn calmly slotted it home. Almost incredibly, Rangers were ahead, but their lead was short-lived. After 52 minutes, a shot by Deans was punched off the line by John Greig, and Connelly stepped forward, heedless of thousands of whistling Rangers fans, to equalise from the spot.

The goal that clinched the game for Rangers was hardly a classic, but it was certainly memorable. Tommy McLean directed a free-kick into the Celtic penalty area, aiming for the head of Derek Johnstone. Johnstone moved forward and headed the ball, which hit a post, rolled tantalisingly along the goal-line before hitting the opposite upright, and was finally poked home from six inches by Tom Forsyth! Forsyth had never scored for Rangers, but if ever there was a time to break his duck, this was it. With 30 minutes remaining, Rangers were ahead, and Celtic seemed to wilt.

Both Conn and MacDonald could have added to the tally as Rangers took control, but it stayed 3–2 and at the final whistle Greig and Parlane were among those seen weeping in a mixture of joy and relief. On the terraces, riotous celebrations heralded the return of the Scottish Cup to Ibrox. Celtic, for their part, had contributed richly to a game which did much to restore the tarnished image of the national game, but this was undoubtedly Rangers' day.

Team: McCloy, Jardine, Mathieson, Greig, Johnstone, A MacDonald, McLean, Forsyth, Parlane, Conn, Young.

RANGERS

After taking over at Rangers, Graeme Souness made a succession of big-money signings, many from south of the border, and quickly re-established the club as a force to be reckoned with. In his first season, Rangers won the League Cup and then their first League title in nine attempts, so expectations were high at the start of the 1987-88 campaign. However, a side blighted by injuries slumped to a poor third in the League, and, worse still, Celtic took seven points out of eight in the season's Old Firm derbies. Rangers ended the year with only a narrow League Cup victory over Aberdeen to celebrate.

This impressive victory in the opening Old Firm game of the new season was, then, particularly sweet. Rangers looked composed and professional in every department, and although Celtic boss Billy McNeill had some justification in his post-match criticism of his defenders, Rangers deserved their win. They established a clear superiority in midfield early in the game, Ray Wilkins, Iain Durrant and Ian Ferguson combining to stifle the talents of Paul McStay, while in defence Terry Butcher and ex-Everton new boy Gary Stevens always looked assured.

Celtic briefly looked like making a match of it, Frank McAvennie opening the scoring after ten minutes when he pounced on a Peter Grant shot which came back off a post. After that, Rangers took over, and before long McCoist had levelled the scores. The best goal of the game followed, an unstoppable 20-yard shot from Wilkins which put Rangers 2-1 up at the interval.

Within a minute of the restart, McCoist had scored again to put the game beyond Celtic, but it was a goal which had even more disastrous consequences for Ian Andrews, the 24-year-old keeper signed from Leicester City just a month before. It was a soft goal, Andrews fluffing a touch over the bar which he should have managed comfortably – but in the days that followed he was unjustly made the scapegoat by both fans and the media for a poor team performance, and would play just four more games for the Parkhead side.

Rangers completed their biggest League win of the season with goals from Englishmen Kevin Drinkell and Mark Walters. They were on their way to the first of an impressive string of League titles which would continue well into the 1990s.

Team: Woods, Stevens, Brown, Gough, Wilkins, Butcher, Drinkell, I Ferguson, McCoist, Durrant, Walters.

LEAGUE CUP RECORD

Introduced just after the war, the League (currently Coca–Cola) Cup was quick to make an appearance in the Ibrox trophy room.

Stage	Opponents	Score
1946-47		
Section B	St Mirren	4-0, 4-0
Section B	Queen's Park	4-2, 1-0
Section B	Morton	3-0, 2-0
Quarter-Final	Dundee U	2-1, 1-1
Semi-Final	Hibernian	3-1
Final	Aberdeen	4-0
1947-48		
Section C	Celtic	2-0, 0-2
Section C	Third Lanark	3-1, 3-0
Section C	Dundee	3-0, 1-1
Quarter-Final	Stenhousemuir	2-0
Semi-Final	Falkirk	0-1
1948-49		
Section A	Clyde	1-1, 3-1
Section A	Hibernian	0-0, 1-0
Section A	Celtic	1-3, 2-1
Quarter-Final	St Mirren	1-0
Semi-Final	Dundee	4-1
Final	Raith Rovers	2-0

Stage	Opponents	Score

1949-50

Section A	Celtic	2-3, 2-0
Section A	St Mirren	5-1, 1-1
Section A	Aberdeen	4-2, 1-1
Quarter-Final	Cowdenbeath	2-3, 3-1
Semi-Final	East Fife	1-2

1950-51

Section D	Morton	2-1, 6-1
Section D	Aberdeen	1-2, 0-2
Section D	Clyde	4-0, 5-1

Rangers did not qualify for Quarter-Final

1951-52

Section D	East Fife	0-0, 4-1
Section D	Aberdeen	2-1, 1-2
Section D	Queen of the South	3-0, 5-2
Quarter-Final	Dunfermline A	0-1, 3-1
Semi-Final	Celtic	3-0
Final	Dundee	2-3

1952-53

Section C	Hearts	0-5, 2-0
Section C	Motherwell	2-0, 3-3
Section C	Aberdeen	3-1, 2-1
Quarter-Final	Third Lanark	0-0, 2-0
Semi-Final	Kilmarnock	0-1

1953-54

Section C	Raith Rovers	4-0, 3-1
Section C	Hearts	4-1, 1-1
Section C	Hamilton A	5-1, 5-0
Quarter-Final	Ayr U	4-2, 2-3
Semi-Final	Partick Thistle	0-2

RANGERS

Stage	Opponents	Score
1954-55		
Section C	Stirling Albion	5-0, 2-0
Section C	Partick Thistle	1-1, 2-1
Section C	Clyde	1-3, 2-1
Quarter-Final	Motherwell	1-2, 1-1
1955-56		
Section 4	Falkirk	5-0, 4-3
Section 4	Queen of the South	2-1, 6-0
Section 4	Celtic	1-4, 4-0
Quarter-Final	Hamilton A	2-1, 8-0
Semi-Final	Aberdeen	1-2
1956-57		
Section 2	East Fife	3-0, 4-1
Section 2	Celtic	1-2, 0-0
Section 2	Aberdeen	6-2, 4-1
Rangers did not qualify for Quarter-Final		
1957-58		
Section 2	St Mirren	6-0, 4-0
Section 2	Partick Thistle	1-0, 0-3
Section 2	Raith Rovers	4-3, 3-4
Quarter-Final	Kilmarnock	1-2, 3-1
Semi-Final	Brechin City	4-0
Final	Celtic	1-7
1958-59		
Section 1	Hearts	3-0, 1-2
Section 1	Raith Rovers	1-3, 6-0
Section 1	Third Lanark	2-2, 3-0
Rangers did not qualify for Quarter-Final		
1959-60		
Section 4	Hibernian	6-1, 5-1
Section 4	Motherwell	1-2, 1-2
Section 4	Dundee	2-0, 3-2
Rangers did not qualify for Quarter-Final		

Stage	Opponents	Score
	1960-61	
Section 2	Partick Thistle	3-1, 4-1
Section 2	Third Lanark	1-2, 3-2
Section 2	Celtic	2-3, 2-1
Quarter-Final	Dundee	1-0, 4-3
Semi-Final	Queen of the South	7-0
Final	Kilmarnock	2-0
	1961-62	
Section 3	Third Lanark	2-0, 5-0
Section 3	Dundee	4-2, 1-1
Section 3	Airdrieonians	2-1, 4-1
Quarter-Final	East Fife	3-1, 3-1
Semi-Final	St Johnstone	3-2
Final	Hearts	1-1, 3-1
	1962-63	
Section 4	Hibernian	4-1, 0-0
Section 4	Third Lanark	5-2, 5-2
Section 4	St Mirren	1-2, 4-0
Quarter-Final	Dumbarton	3-1, 1-1
Semi-Final	Kilmarnock	2-3
	1963-64	
Section 4	Celtic	3-0, 3-0
Section 4	Queen of the South	5-2, 5-2
Section 4	Kilmarnock	4-1, 2-2
Quarter-Final	East Fife	1-1, 2-0
Semi-Final	Berwick R	3-1
Final	Morton	5-0
	1964-65	
Section 1	Aberdeen	4-0, 4-3
Section 1	St Mirren	0-0, 6-2
Section 1	St Johnstone	9-1, 3-1
Quarter-Final	Dunfermline A	3-0, 2-2
Semi-Final	Dundee U	2-1
Final	Celtic	2-1

RANGERS

Stage	Opponents	Score
1965-66		
Section 2	Hearts	2-4, 1-0
Section 2	Clyde	3-0, 3-1
Section 2	Aberdeen	0-2, 4-0
Quarter-Final	Airdrieonians	5-1, 4-0
Semi-Final	Kilmarnock	6-4
Final	Celtic	1-2
1966-67		
Section 2	Hibernian	1-0, 2-3
Section 2	Stirling Albion	8-0, 1-1
Section 2	Kilmarnock	0-0, 1-0
Quarter-Final	Ayr U	1-1, 3-0
Semi-Final	Aberdeen	2-2, 2-0
Final	Celtic	0-1
1967-68		
Section 2	Aberdeen	1-1, 3-0
Section 2	Celtic	1-1, 1-3
Section 2	Dundee U	1-0, 3-0
Rangers did not qualify for Quarter-Final		
1968-69		
Section 4	Celtic	0-2, 0-1
Section 4	Partick Thistle	5-1, 2-1
Section 4	Morton	2-0, 5-0
Rangers did not qualify for Quarter-Final		
1969-70		
Section 1	Raith Rovers	3-2, 3-3
Section 1	Celtic	2-1, 0-1
Section 1	Airdrieonians	3-0, 3-0
Rangers did not qualify for Quarter-Final		

RANGERS

Stage	Opponents	Score
1970-71		
Section 2	Dunfermline A	4-1, 6-0
Section 2	Motherwell	2-0, 2-0
Section 2	Morton	0-0, 2-0
Quarter-Final	Hibernian	3-1, 3-1
Semi-Final	Cowdenbeath	2-0
Final	Celtic	1-0
1971-72		
Section 4	Celtic	0-2, 0-3
Section 4	Ayr U	4-0, 4-0
Section 4	Morton	2-0, 1-0
Rangers did not qualify for Quarter-Final		
1972-73		
Section 3	Clydebank	2-0, 5-0
Section 3	St Mirren	4-0, 1-4
Section 3	Ayr U	2-1, 2-1
Quarter-Final	Stenhousemuir	5-0, 1-2
Semi-Final	St Johnstone	1-1, 2-0
Final	Hibernian	0-1
1973-74		
Section 1	Falkirk	3-1, 5-1
Section 1	Arbroath	2-1, 3-0
Section 1	Celtic	1-2, 3-1
Round 2	Dumbarton	6-0, 2-1
Quarter-Final	Hibernian	2-0, 0-0
Semi-Final	Celtic	1-3
1974-75		
Section 2	St Johnstone	3-2, 6-3
Section 2	Hibernian	1-3, 0-1
Section 2	Dundee	2-0, 4-0
Rangers did not qualify for Quarter-Final		

Stage	Opponents	Score
1975-76		
Section 1	Airdrieonians	6-1, 2-1
Section 1	Clyde	1-0, 6-0
Section 1	Motherwell	1-1, 2-2
Quarter-Final	Queen of the South	1-0, 2-2
Semi-Final	Montrose	5-1
Final	Celtic	1-0
1976-77		
Section 4	St Johnstone	5-0, 1-0
Section 4	Hibernian	1-1, 3-0
Section 4	Montrose	4-0, 3-0
Quarter-Final	Clydebank	3-3, 1-1, 0-0, 2-1
Semi-Final	Aberdeen	1-5
1977-78		
Round 2	St Johnstone	3-1, 3-0
Round 3	Aberdeen	6-1, 1-3
Quarter-Final	Dunfermline A	3-1, 3-1
Semi-Final	Forfar A	5-2
Final	Celtic	2-1
1978-79		
Round 1	Albion R	3-0, 1-0
Round 2	Forfar A	3-0, 4-1
Round 3	St Mirren	3-2, 0-0
Quarter-Final	Arbroath	1-0, 2-1
Semi-Final	Celtic	3-2
Final	Aberdeen	2-1
1979-80		
Round 2	Clyde	2-1, 4-0
Round 3	Aberdeen	1-3, 0-2
1980-81		
Round 2	Forfar A	2-0, 3-1
Round 3	Aberdeen	1-0, 1-3

Stage	Opponents	Score
1981-82		
Section 2	Morton	1-1, 1-0
Section 2	Dundee	4-1, 2-1
Section 2	Raith Rovers	6-1, 3-1
Quarter-Final	Brechin City	4-0, 1-0
Semi-Final	St Mirren	2-2, 2-1
Final	Dundee U	2-1
1982-83		
Section 3	Hibernian	1-1, 0-0
Section 3	Airdrieonians	3-1, 2-1
Section 3	Clydebank	4-1, 3-2
Quarter-Final	Kilmarnock	6-1, 6-0
Semi-Final	Hearts	2-0, 2-1
Final	Celtic	1-2
1983-84		
Round 2	Queen of the South	4-0, 4-1
Round 3 Section 2	Clydebank	4-0, 3-0
Round 3 Section 2	Hearts	3-0, 2-0
Round 3 Section 2	St Mirren	5-0, 1-0
Semi-Final	Dundee U	1-1, 2-0
Final	Celtic	3-2
1984-85		
Round 2	Falkirk	1-0
Round 3	Raith Rovers	4-0
Quarter-Final	Cowdenbeath	3-1
Semi-Final	Meadowbank	4-0, 1-1
Final	Dundee U	1-0
1985-86		
Round 2	Clyde	5-0
Round 3	Forfar A	2-2
Rangers won 6-5 on penalties		
Quarter-Final	Hamilton A	2-1
Semi-Final	Hibernian	0-2, 1-0

Stage	Opponents	Score
1986-87		
Round 2	Stenhousemuir	4-1
Round 3	East Fife	0-0
Rangers won 5-4 on penalties		
Quarter-Final	Dundee	3-1
Semi-Final	Dundee U	2-1
Final	Celtic	2-1
1987-88		
Round 2	Stirling Albion	2-1
Round 3	Dunfermline A	4-1
Quarter-Final	Hearts	4-1
Semi-Final	Motherwell	3-1
Final	Aberdeen	3-3
Rangers won 5-3 on penalties		
1988-89		
Round 2	Clyde	3-0
Round 3	Clydebank	6-0
Quarter-Final	Dundee	4-1
Semi-Final	Hearts	3-0
Final	Aberdeen	3-2
1989-90		
Round 2	Arbroath	4-0
Round 3	Morton	2-1
Quarter-Final	Hamilton A	3-0
Semi-Final	Dunfermline A	5-0
Final	Aberdeen	1-2
1990-91		
Round 2	East Stirling	5-0
Round 3	Kilmarnock	1-0
Quarter-Final	Raith Rovers	6-2
Semi-Final	Aberdeen	1-0
Final	Celtic	2-1

Stage	Opponents	Score
1991-92		
Round 2	Queen's Park	6-0
Round 3	Partick Thistle	2-0
Quarter-Final	Hearts	1-0
Semi-Final	Hibernian	0-1
1992-93		
Round 2	Dumbarton	5-0
Round 3	Stranraer	5-0
Quarter-Final	Dundee U	3-2
Semi-Final	St Johnstone	3-1
Final	Aberdeen	2-1
1993-94		
Round 2	Dumbarton	1-0
Round 3	Dunfermline A	2-0
Quarter-Final	Aberdeen	2-1
Semi-Final	Celtic	1-0
Final	Hibernian	2-1
1994-95		
Round 2	Arbroath	6-1
Round 3	Falkirk	1-2
1995-96		
Round 2	Morton	3-0
Round 3	Stirling Albion	3-2
Quarter-Final	Celtic	1-0
Semi-Final	Aberdeen	1-2
1996-97		
Round 2	Clydebank	3-0
Round 3	Ayr U	3-1
Quarter-Final	Hibernian	4-0
Semi-Final	Dunfermline A	6-1
Final	Hearts	4-3

RANGERS

Stage	Opponents	Score
1997-98		
Round 2	Hamilton A	1-0
Round 3	Falkirk	4-1
Quarter-Final	Dundee U	0-1

League Cup Record Club By Club

Opposition	P	W	D	L	F-A
Aberdeen	35	19	4	12	73-56
Airdrieonians	10	10	—	—	34-7
Albion R	2	2	—	—	4-0
Arbroath	6	6	—	—	18-3
Ayr U	9	7	1	1	25-9
Berwick R	1	1	—	—	3-1
Brechin City	3	3	—	—	9-0
Celtic	40	20	2	18	58-59
Clyde	14	12	1	1	43-9
Clydebank	12	9	3	—	36-8
Cowdenbeath	4	3	—	1	10-5
Dumbarton	6	5	1	—	18-3
Dundee	16	13	2	1	44-17
Dundee U	12	9	2	1	20-9
Dunfermline A	12	10	1	1	41-9
East Fife	10	6	3	1	21-7
East Stirling	1	1	—	—	5-0
Falkirk	8	6	—	2	23-9
Forfar A	6	5	1	—	19-6
Hamilton A	7	7	—	—	26-3
Hearts	18	13	2	3	39-20
Hibernian	25	13	6	6	43-20
Kilmarnock	13	8	2	3	34-15
Meadowbank	2	1	1	—	5-1
Montrose	3	3	—	—	12-1
Morton	15	13	2	—	37-4
Motherwell	11	4	4	3	19-14
Partick Thistle	10	7	1	2	20-11
Queen of the South	11	10	1	—	44-10
Queen's Park	3	3	—	—	11-2
Raith Rovers	13	10	1	2	48-20
St Johnstone	12	11	1	—	42-12
St Mirren	19	13	4	2	53-15
Stenhousemuir	4	3	—	1	12-3
Stirling Albion	6	5	1	—	21-4
Stranraer	1	1	—	—	5-0
Third Lanark	12	9	2	1	34-11

THE FILES

Ibrox managers have mostly been long-servers. Here's a guide to who won what – and when.

Bill Struth
1920–54

Honours: Division One Champions	1920–21, 1922–23, 1923–24, 1924–25, 1926–27, 1927–28, 1928–29, 1929–30, 1930–31, 1932–33, 1933–34, 1934–35, 1936–37, 1938–39, 1946–47, 1948–49, 1949–50, 1952–53
FA Cup Winners	1927–28, 1929–30, 1931–32, 1933–34, 1934–35, 1935–36, 1947–48, 1948–49, 1949–50, 1952–53
FA Cup Runners-up	1920–21, 1921–22, 1928–29
League Cup Winners	1946–47, 1948–49
League Cup Runners-up	1951–52

Bill Struth, a former player, became the club's first manager after secretary William Wilton drowned in 1920 – and by the time of his retirement had amassed an impressive 18 League titles, reached ten Cup Finals and two League Cup Finals. Three consecutive Scottish Cup wins from 1934–36 were the highlight of his reign, while the 1948–49 season brought an historic 'treble' of League, Cup and League Cup thanks to the so-called 'Iron Curtain' defence which remained virtually unchanged from 1946 to 1953. The former athletics trainer stepped down in 1954 due to ill health, but would never be forgotten.

Scot Symon
1954–67

Honours:	Division One Champions	1955–56, 1956–57, 1958–59, 1960–61, 1962–63, 1963–64
	FA Cup Winners	1959–60, 1961–62, 1962–63, 1963–64, 1965–66
	League Cup Winners	1960–61, 1961–62, 1963–64, 1964–65
	League Cup Runners–up	1957–58, 1965–66, 1966–67
	Euopean Cup Winners' Cup Runners–up	1960–61, 1966–67

Scot Symon, a Rangers player from 1938–47 who'd appeared once for Scotland, had already proved his worth by taking lowly East Fife to three League cups and a Second Division Championship before coming to Ibrox: a season at Preston in–between had proved less successful. The club dominated domestically, and reached two European Finals without clinching a Cup, but having replaced a legend in Bill Struth the rise of another, Jock Stein across the city, overshadowed him and he paid the penalty of Celtic's success in Scotland and Europe in 1967, giving way to his former assistant Davie White.

David White
1967–69
Honours: FA Cup Runners–up   1968–69

White would be the shortest–serving Rangers boss, his reign lasting barely two years. He needed to win back the League title to have any chance of a lasting career in the job, but the former Clyde midfielder was unable to bring home the bacon with Celtic off and running on their nine in a row sequence. He bowed to the inevitable and resigned after Rangers crashed out of Europe to Polish club Gornik.

Willie Waddell
1969–72
Honours: FA Cup Runners–up   1970–71
         League Cup Winners   1970–71
         European Cup Winners' Cup
         Winners   1971–72

As well as being a celebrated former player, Willie Waddell had already made his mark in management by taking lowly Kilmarnock to the Championship in 1965 and had retired to become a sports journalist when the call came. He made an immediate mark by bringing back the League Cup in 1971 and after leading Rangers to European glory in Barcelona's Nou Camp Stadium in 1972 was to step upstairs, handing over responsibility for playing matters to coach Jock Wallace. The latter's success was certainly built on Waddell's foundations.

Jock Wallace
1972–78 and 1983–86
Honours: Division One Champions   1974–75, 1975–76,
                                       1977–78

       FA Cup Winners   1972–73, 1975–76,
                                  1977–78

       FA Cup Runners-up   1976–77
       League Cup Winners   1975–76, 1977–78,
                                      1983–84, 1984–85

Stepping up from coach, Jock Wallace was able to finally break the Celtic spell, leading the Gers to three titles in 1975, 1976 and 1978. The last two were Trebles, proving that Rangers were not only masters of the Glasgow scene but kings of Scottish football. A former goalkeeper and soldier, Jock's training methods were uncompromising but brought results. He left for Leicester City, his team having grown old without suitable youngsters having emerged to take the veterans' places.

Wallace's return to Ibrox for a second spell (having meanwhile resurfaced north of the border as manager of Motherwell) was not to prove as profitable as the first. Indeed Rangers' board had been turned down by Jim McLean (Dundee United) and Alex Ferguson (Aberdeen), their first choices. Rangers ended 1985–86 in fifth place, their equal worst postwar showing, with fewer points than games. Despite two League Cups, Wallace had clearly proved unequal to the task of re-establishing Rangers as the top dogs they had been under his earlier rule.

John Greig
1978–83

Honours:	FA Cup Winners	1978–79, 1980–81
	FA Cup Runners-up	1979–80, 1981–82, 1982–83
	League Cup Winners	1978–79, 1981–82
	League Cup Runners-up	1982–83

John Greig, a legend on the playing front over 18 years at Ibrox, had the misfortune of taking charge as manager just when a century of history was about to be rewritten as the 'New Firm' of Aberdeen and Dundee United challenged Glasgow dominance. Five years in the Ibrox hot seat brought cups but no League title, and Greig did the decent thing and resigned after the first nine games of the 1983–84 season. He may in retrospect have suffered, as available funds went into rebuilding Ibrox and not so much the first team squad.

Graeme Souness
1986–91

Honours:	Division One Champions	1986–87, 1988–89, 1989–90
	FA Cup Runners-up	1988–89
	League Cup Winners	1986–87, 1987–88, 1988–89, 1990–91
	League Cup Runners-up	1989–90

A boardroom takeover in January 1986 brought in its wake the first player-manager in Rangers' history. Graeme Souness, who'd captained Liverpool to Championships before going to Italy, found a playing role too high-pressure to sustain, but won immediate success in his first season in management, aided by a stream of players from south of the border. A Championship and League Cup Double was an impressive start, but he departed on a high after title number four, combined with a League Cup win against Celtic. In 1989, he'd ended Rangers' 'no Catholics' policy by signing ex-Celtic striker Maurice Johnston – another reason to remember him.

Walter Smith
1991–(97)

Honours:	Division One Champions	1990–91, 1991–92, 1992–93, 1993–94, 1994–95, 1995–96, 1996–97
	FA Cup Winners	1991–92, 1992–93, 1995–96
	FA Cup Runners–up	1993–94
	League Cup Winners	1992–93, 1993–94, 1996–97

If Souness's decision to return to his spiritual home, Anfield, had been an unpleasant shock, Rangers directors didn't have far to look for a replacement: despite a lack of previous managerial form, they believed – rightly – Walter Smith was capable of continuing the success story. The players he brought in included Gascoigne and Laudrup, two all-time greats, and the titles continued to clock up with satisfactory regularity.

Yet the major goal, success in Europe, seemed beyond Smith, despite considerable outlay on players, and after their 1997 exit, the club announced he'd be stepping down (or up) at the end of a season which saw Rangers challenge for their tenth consecutive Championship.

BEST SEASON 2

**You can't do better than win the Treble –
and the Rangers team of 1975-76, under the
managership of Jock Wallace, would do this
not once but twice in three years.**

From the August kick-off in front of nearly 70,000 that
saw Celtic dispatched 2-1 to the slightly anti-climactic
scoreless draw with Dundee United the following May,
the Ibrox turnstiles were clicking away merrily as Rangers
celebrated the first season of the new, 10-club Premier
Division that replaced the old 18-club regime in the best
possible style.

The really impressive phase of the season began in
December with a win against Ayr on the 13th. It wouldn't
prove unlucky for Rangers, for they remained unbeaten from
then to the rest of the season. In domestic terms, that is –
sadly, they'd bow out of the European Cup to St Etienne,
losing at Ibrox as well as away. But who could be greedy when
the League Cup Final saw yet another defeat of Celtic? The
new system saw the clubs meet four times in the League, and
since those games ended with two Rangers wins and two
draws there could be no doubting who held the balance of
power in Glasgow.

Up front, the two Dereks, Parlane and Johnstone
hammered in the goals from crosses supplied by the two
Macs, McLean and McKean. Forsyth and Jackson were an
imposing central defensive barrier flanked by Jardine and
veteran club captain John Greig, now at left-back as his pace
had deserted him, but retaining a place in the side as its only
ever-present. His expert reading of the game made up for any
lack of pace.

The Scottish FA Cup was secured in May with a 3-1 win over Hearts, no replays having been required in disposing of East Fife, Aberdeen, Queen of the South and Motherwell by an imperious 15-3 aggregate. The title had already been clinched with three games to go. Not that it had been a foregone conclusion: Celtic went into 1976 with a three-point lead at the top, but the aforementioned unbeaten run was to see them off in style.

Frankly the only disappointment was not wining the Glasgow Cup – but that was only because fixture congestion dictated the Final be held over to the start of the following season. And guess what? They won that too, 3-1 against Celtic. But 1976-77 saw more or less the same team come away with no more silverware than that locally-contested trophy. Funny game, football!

1975-76 LEAGUE RECORD		
Opponents	**Home**	**Away**
Aberdeen	1-0	0-1
Aberdeen	2-1	0-0
Ayr United	3-0	0-3
Ayr United	2-1	1-0
Celtic	2-1	1-1
Celtic	1-0	0-0
Dundee	2-1	0-0
Dundee	3-0	1-1
Dundee United	4-1	0-0
Dundee United	0-0	1-0
Hearts	1-2	2-0
Hearts	3-1	2-1
Hibernian	1-1	1-2
Hibernian	2-0	3-0
Motherwell	3-2	1-2
Motherwell	2-1	1-0
St Johnstone	2-0	5-1
St Johnstone	4-0	3-0

THE GROUNDS

The proud name of Glasgow Rangers is always linked with that of the Ibrox Stadium, and indeed has been for the last 110 years. But did you know that there have been not one but two Ibroxes – or that the club's first ground was actually Glasgow Green?

By the time they arrived at the first Ibrox in 1887, the Gers had already played at two more grounds, Burnbank (1875) and Kinning Park (1876). This last venue, situated in the city's shipbuilding heart a mile to the east of Ibrox, was ideally situated for gathering support from the working classes, but proved very limited in capacity. The same thing happened at their new home and the final year of the century saw them develop a new ground beside the first. The original venue was gradually overshadowed by the 40,000-capacity newcomer taking shape nearby – one that boasted a two-storey pavilion and a stand.

Rangers expanded their new ground to a capacity of just under 70,000 with the hope of gaining a share of Scotland's international matches. But terracing built at the west end of the ground proved inadequate, and collapsed during an England–Scotland fixture on 5 April 1902. Twenty-five lives were lost and nearly 600 spectators injured.

Earth banking replaced the former iron and wood framework that had proved so fatally flawed, and when Ibrox's capacity rose from the post–disaster 25,000 limit, it did so safely under the direction of famous architect Archibald

Leitch. Success on the pitch funded a new 10,000-seater stand – the proceeds of Rangers' first ever League and Cup Double in 1928. Eleven years later Rangers opened their doors to a record number of spectators – 118,567 – for Celtic's annual visit.

Floodlights were installed in 1953, and the North Side and East End terracing were shielded from the elements in the 1960s. Sadly, the Old Firm game of 2 January 1971 brought a second Ibrox disaster, 66 people losing their lives when crush barriers that ran along the centre of Ibrox's Stairway 13 buckled. As in 1902, though, the event was to mark the beginning of redevelopment with safety in mind. This was so extensive, in fact, that the club had to play the 1972–73 season at Hampden Park.

A major £6 million redevelopment started in 1977, based on Germany's Dortmund Stadium: the South Stand, Archibald Leitch's creation, was retained, while its Enclosure retained some terracing, but elsewhere it was seating all the way with two matching edifices, the Copland Road and Broomloan Road Stands, replacing the East and West terracing (Stairway 13 disappearing as a result).

The Centenary Stand which had replaced the North Enclosure was itself superseded by the 10,300-capacity North Stand in 1981, its opening revealing an all-new Ibrox with a 'mere' 45,000 capacity. Behind the scenes, computers and closed-circuit TV helped ensure that the stadium that had suffered two crowd disasters would henceforth be one of the safest sporting venues in the world.

Ibrox Stadium entered the new millenium with an all-seated capacity of nearly 50,000 – around one quarter of that famous 1939 record attendance, but considerably safer and more luxuriously appointed. It was a ground fit for champions, giving the team much to live up to and the fans the ideal environment in which to watch their heroes. It was all a long way from Glasgow Green in 1872…

THROUGH THE YEARS
JULY

1969
July
30

Gordan Petric is born today in Belgrade, Yugoslavia. He arrived in Scotland in 1993 from Partizan Belgrade, countryman Ivan Golac having been first to notice his cool defensive talents, and a £1 million move to Ibrox followed two years later.

1972
July
29

Rangers win their first ever match in the Drybrough Cup, a pre-season curtain-raiser. Stirling Albion are easily beaten 3–1, Stein scoring twice, but the plot goes awry four days later when Hibernian end Rangers interest in the competition by a 3–0 margin at Easter Road. Rangers would go out to the same opposition in 1973 but reached the Final in 1974.

1980
July
30

Partick Thistle are beaten 3-1 at Ibrox in the newly revived Anglo-Scottish Cup. But worse is to come as the Jags win 3-2 in the second leg and, when English opposition is met in the form of lowly Chesterfield, Rangers flop out of this less than prestigious competition on a 4-1 aggregate.

1985
July
29

Jock Wallace's last season in charge is given a false dawn by the second of two big pre-season wins, a 6-0 against Caledonian Thistle following a 5-1 against Ross County. Both matches featured the regular first team against non-League opposition, but the regular Premier Division fare would prove less rewarding.

1995
July
30

Rangers win the Ibrox International Trophy at the second time of asking, beating Sampdoria (who had turned them over the previous season) 2-0 in the Final, after trouncing Steaua Bucharest 4-0.

ATTENDANCES

Rangers are the game's most noted crowd-pullers north of the border, where every game's a Cup Final.

The visit of one of Glasgow's big two will, more often than not, be the highlight not only of most teams' seasons but also their bank managers'! Attendances tend to get a much-needed hike when Rangers appear — and, even though they pay two annual visits to each Premier division club these days, the Gers regularly inspire the highest crowd figures.

The Old Firm games still bring out the fans like no other — and it's symptomatic of that fixture's evergreen status that reserve matches over the years have been known to pull in crowds of up to 20,000. Only one of 1996–97's four first-team clashes came up short of the 50,000 mark, and that by a mere 268 souls. Maybe they sneaked in under the turnstiles...

Two derbies that preceded World War II are specially notable. On 1 January 1938 the crowd at Celtic was estimated at 85,000: eyewitness accounts suggest up to 7,000 more attended. Rangers then showed that they could do anything at least as well as their rivals when 118,567 packed through

Ibrox's gates a year later, a record attendance for a League game in Britain being established. Crowds like this, of course, are now things of the past.

Aside from Celtic, no fewer than 14 Scottish League clubs have registered their highest figures when facing the boys in blue. Way back in November 1908, Clyde somehow managed to pack 52,000 into their Broadwood Stadium to watch a League game, while 14 years later Partick Thistle welcomed their near neighbours and 49,838 fans to Firhill.

Hearts opened their Tynecastle doors in February 1932 and celebrated a ground record with 53,496 – though the visitors came away 1-0 victors in a Scottish FA Cup tie. Albion Rovers' 27,381 was also registered for a Scottish Cup game, the Second Round in February 1938, while Celtic's 85,000 – or 92,000, as previously discussed – which occurred just a month earlier remains their record today. Rangers came out top on that occasion by a 2-1 margin.

The postwar era saw Rangers break even more attendance records. Cowdenbeath were delighted to usher 25,586 for a League Cup Quarter-Final in September 1949, while the early 1950s saw three opponents post records on playing host to the blues. Arbroath and Motherwell did theirs within a month in the Third and Fourth Rounds of the FA Cup in

1952, while Dundee's 43,024 flocked the following season. Only Motherwell managed a result.

A Second Round Cup draw against then non-League Ross County must have caused Rangers fans a few collywobbles in February 1966. An 8,000 crowd at Victoria Park saw the Gers pass through 2-0 – not comfortably, perhaps, but Scot Symon's team went all the way to take the Cup after a single-goal Final defeat of Celtic. It was a very different story the following year when 13,365 delirious Berwick fans packed out Berwick's Shielfield Park to see the local heroes (with one Jock Wallace in goal) knock out the holders in the very First Round with a single-goal win.

Dear little Forfar, the Loons to their long-suffering fans, began the following decade in promising style, their record 10,800 crowd being registered in February 1970 as they flocked to see their team play Rangers in the Cup's Second Round. Unfortunately the Station Park faithful witnessed a 7-0 drubbing, John Greig registering a double.

There have been occasions when Rangers have been watched by abnormally small crowds. Only 1,781 saw them face ASK Vorwaerts in a November 1961 European Cup tie, but that was because the East Germans were refused entry visas and it was played in Sweden. At Ibrox, a rare low crowd of 11,000

was recorded in September 1983 when the Gers played host to Malta's Valetta in the Cup Winners' Cup. With the home team already 8-0 up, an anti-climax was perhaps inevitable – but those who showed saw 10 goals rattled in without reply!

More high attendance records are unlikely to fall in these days of all-seater stadia. There's little doubt, though, that the visit of Glasgow Rangers, whether on League duty or in either Cup, will remain a highlight of nearly every club's sporting calendar. A remarkably large number of loyal season-ticket holders ensure the attendance at Ibrox rarely, if ever, falls below the 40,000 mark – and, on six occasions in 1996-97's League campaign, broke the half-century. And that's music to David Murray's ears as he funds the spending that ensures those who come will be royally entertained...

DREAM TEAM 2

The Souness era was well in swing by 1988–89. And by bringing all three domestic trophies back to Ibrox, he proved himself one of the great managers – thanks to this dream team.

Goalkeeper   **Chris Woods**

English international keeper who might still have been at Ibrox had not the need for home-qualified players in Europe won out. Gave way to Nicky Walker for a dozen games but still undeniably first choice.

Right–back   **Gary Stevens**

Reliable, cultured defender signed from Everton, where he won full England honours. Missed just one game in all competitions, but his back–pass arguably gave Celtic the Cup. Returned to Merseyside with Tranmere in '94.

Left–back   **Stuart Munro**

Signed for just £15,000 from Alloa, Stuart saw off many supposed replacements, clocking up 180 games in a blue shirt before moving south to Blackburn and Bristol City. Dependable.

Central defender   **Richard Gough**

What more needs be said? Captain courageous Gough formed a formidable central defensive barrier with Butcher, helping a team that had finished third become the new season's Champions.

Midfielder   Ray Wilkins

Much-travelled England midfielder made Glasgow his next stop after Paris and won many friends playing in the unusual Number 5 shirt. Now manages Fulham after an unfortunate first move upstairs at QPR where he signed Mark Hateley.

Central defender   Terry Butcher

Man mountain Butcher became as integral to Souness's defence as his national side, and despite an unhappy end to his spell at Ibrox remains north of the border today as a media commentator. Missed just two games in the season, having come back from a broken leg.

Centre-forward   Kevin Drinkell

Top scorer in the 1988-89 season in both League and Cup, the ex-Norwich man wasn't one of Rangers' biggest names but was never afraid to put himself about. Played just four times the following season before being sent to Coventry as Johnston and McCoist got the nod.

Midfielder   Ian Ferguson

Scoring the winning goal for St Mirren in the Scottish Cup made Fergie a million-pound man, and he repaid the fee with interest, scoring vital goals from his midfield berth, including one in the League Cup Final.

Midfielder   **Derek Ferguson**

Not the controversial £4 million signing Duncan but a skilful midfielder who was a first-team regular for one and a half seasons. As with his namesake, though, suspensions proved a problem and he ended up with Hearts.

Midfielder   **Graeme Souness**

By this time the player-manager had scaled his own appearances down to that of substitute but he deserves a place in his own team for the inspiration and drive he gave them whether from the bench or the middle of the park. Now manager of Benfica following spells at Liverpool, Galatasaray, Southampton and Torino.

Winger   **Mark Walters**

Gifted yet erratic winger who was on the fringes of the international scene with England, and who reckons leaving Ibrox for Anfield (with Souness) the biggest mistake of his career.

RFC TRIVIA QUIZ

Test your Ibrox knowledge.
Answers on page 190–191.

1   What is Rangers' motto?

2   Who was Rangers' first player–manager?

3   Which former Rangers midfielder is now manager of Fulham?

4   From which club was Marco Negri signed for £3.5 million?

5   What nationality is Staale Sensaas?

6   Who is the only man to manage Rangers twice?

7   Which combative 1980s midfielder also played for Millwall, Reading and Fulham?

8   Which club does former forward Kevin Drinkell now manage?

9   In what position did Rangers finish in Graeme Souness's second season in charge?

10   Who is chairman of Rangers?

11   Which architect was the brains behind Ibrox?

12   Which club knocked Rangers out of Europe in 1997?

13   Who did Andy Goram replace in Rangers' goal?

14   Which illustrious defender returned to Rangers in
      late 1997?

15   Which Rangers manager's christian names were
      James Scotland?

16   Which former Ranger has won Championships as
      manager north and south of the border?

17   Which Ranger was sent home from the World Cup
      in disgrace?

18   Where was Michael Laudrup born?

19   How many Scottish FA Cups did Rangers win
      in the 1980s?

20   How many seasons did Trevor Francis play
      for Rangers?

21   Name the full-back (now with Tranmere) who joined
      Rangers in 1988.

22   Which Rangers captain was the only one to hold
      European silverware aloft?

23   Which player was sold to Marseille in 1991 and
      returned a year later?

24   Why was the Old Firm Cup Final of 1909 abandoned?

25 Which Ranger won his 50th Scottish cap against Australia in 1996?

26 With which club did Rangers share the first Scottish League Championship?

27 Which nationality was keeper Bonni Ginzburg?

28 To which club was David McPherson sold,/bought then sold again?

29 What nationality is Gordan Petric?

30 With which club did Paul Gascoigne begin his professional career?

31 Which 1990s defender rejoiced in the nickname Elvis?

32 How many seasons did Graeme Souness spend in the Ibrox hot seat?

33 Which Ibrox legend died in 1995, aged just 39?

34 Which Ranger scored against another Ranger at Euro '96?

35 Which top English team did Rangers beat in the 1992-93 European Cup?

36 Which Ranger, now a media pundit, won medals in four different positions?

37 Which Ranger, also a media pundit, runs a Scottish hotel?

38   In which (pre–1998) year did Rangers last *not* win the title?

39   Which club did Walter Smith manage before taking charge at Rangers?

40   Which Rangers striker played for Spurs, Chelsea, East Fife and Hibs?

THROUGH THE YEARS
AUGUST

1876

August

Rangers moved ground this month from Burnbank to Kinning Park, south of the Clyde and the former home of Clydesdale. Next stop was the first Ibrox in 1887.

1890

August

16

The first ever Rangers League goal was scored against Hearts – not by a man in blue but an own goal by Jimmy Adams.

1986

August

9

Player-manager Graeme Souness is sent off in his first League game in a blue shirt, against Hibernian. He would eventually decide to hang up his boots after further brushes with authority.

1991

August

10

Walter Smith celebrates his first full season in charge with a 6–0 opening-day win against St Johnstone. Mark Hateley (3) and Mo Johnston (2) grab the lion's share of the goals as Ally McCoist is kept in reserve.

1994

August

6

Rangers beat Manchester United 1–0 in the Ibrox International Tournament, Eric Cantona being sent off for a rash challenge on Steve Pressley. Alex Ferguson, himself an ex-Ranger, claims fans are 'stuck in the past' for abusing his side.

1995

August

4

The Metropolitan Police police bar Rangers from playing Gary Mabbutt's testimonial at Spurs, originally scheduled for today, due to trouble at Sunderland the last time supporters crossed the border. Mabbutt, a great mate of Richard Gough from their time together in the centre of the White Hart Lane defence, is understandably 'disappointed'.

TRANSFERS

There was a time when Rangers were not known for splashing the cash: indeed, a number of players, most notably Jim Baxter, left the club in search of richer pickings elsewhere. But all that changed in 1968 as new management searched for new glory – and the result was the arrival at Ibrox of Colin Stein.

Not only did Rangers have to match the money being offered by clubs south of the border, they had to persuade Hibernian to sell their star striker to a club that quite likely would use his gifts against them to maintain their position as one of the 'Old Firm'. It wasn't a recipe guaranteed to delight the Easter Road faithful. A sweetener was therefore necessary in the shape of winger Quinton Young – but even so the £100,000 that was obliged to change hands marked the first time a player had been transferred for six figures in Scotland.

Stein repaid the investment with 60 League goals in 112 games – a return of better than one goal in two. Goalscorers, if not home-produced, have typically cost the most money – though Ally McCoist was a bargain for £150,000, having 'devalued' from £400,000 during the two barren seasons he spent at Sunderland.

When it comes to transfer dealing, though, few can beat Graeme Souness who waved the Rangers chequebook under the noses of a mind-boggling number of players from all points of the compass. He also ensured that Rangers, having been the first Scottish club to spend £100,000, were the first to drop a million, but when you're talking about Richard Gough no one can say the money was wasted. Trevor Steven upped the record to £1.525 million, but was a proven England international sold to Marseille for a profit, while sums in excess of £2 and £4 million respectively have been invested in the prodigious talents of Brian Laudrup and Paul Gascoigne.

While dealing with foreign players can be a lottery, Rangers rarely accept a loss on players purchased in the domestic market. That said, the likes of Gordon Durie (£1.2 million) and Andy Goram (£1 million), both reaching the later years of their careers, are unlikely to recoup the outlay when they finally wave a sad goodbye to Ibrox. Even so, the club will have had their money's worth in long and loyal service.

On the other hand, Duncan Ferguson's short and controversial stay at Ibrox was financially rewarding for the club. His arrival from Dundee United for very nearly £4 million, then a British record, was followed by just 14 League games, six of those as sub, which yielded two goals. He also established himself as something of a hot-head both on and off the pitch, and police action followed a clash with Raith's Jock McStay. The renewed form of Mark Hateley, the man 'Big Dunc' had been tipped to replace, meant he could be sold on to Everton, then in need of a commanding figure – and because he hadn't played enough games to trigger an additional payment to his former club, canny Walter Smith made a profit.

A player, though, is only worth what a club is prepared to pay for him. With that in mind, the last word should go to Dundee United's Maurice Malpas. 'Rangers paid £2 million for Brian Laudrup,' he commented. 'How can Duncan be worth double?' Take a bow, Walter Smith...

WORST SEASON 2

However disappointing it turned out to be, 1964–65 wasn't a totally trophyless season, Rangers managing to retain the League Cup. But with that failing to carry a European place with it, their finishing fifth was the worst performance since 1926, when they'd been placed sixth, and meant no foreign excursions in the campaign ahead – the first time since season 1957–58.

The previous season had brought a Treble, the first in 15 years, but the great Rangers team of the early 1960s was ageing and not enough had been done to bring in new blood. Furthermore Jim Baxter, the side's fabled playmaker, broke his leg playing against Rapid Vienna in December and would be sorely missed.

The season got off to a bad start, with just two wins in eight games. The ninth and tenth saw the dam explode with 7-0 and 6-1 wins against the minnows of St Mirren and Clyde, but inconsistency dogged the team and the second half of the season without Baxter brought draws, losses and wins in equal measure.

The League Cup win – 2-1 against Celtic, both goals from the prolific Gerry Forrest – was sweet as these victories always are. But apart from Forrest (30 goals), only Wilson got into double figures. Defenders Provan, Greig and McKinnon all turned in ever-present League records, and while it seemed for a time that European Cup glory might be on the cards, a

3-1 defeat in the San Siro against Inter Milan proved just too much to claw back and they went out at the Quarter-Final stage.

Ominously, Celtic chose the end of the season to change their manager, the return of former player Jock Stein presaging a period when green, not blue, would be the predominant colour in Glasgow. And though Scot Symon was retained until the 1967–68 season, this was undoubtedly the end of an era at Ibrox too.

1964–65 LEAGUE RECORD		
Opponents	**Home**	**Away**
Aberdeen	2-2	0-2
Airdrieonians	9-2	4-0
Celtic	1-0	1-3
Clyde	6-1	3-0
Dundee	4-0	1-4
Dundee United	0-1	3-1
Dunfermline A	0-0	1-3
Falkirk	6-1	5-0
Hearts	1-1	1-1
Hibernian	2-4	0-1
Kilmarnock	1-1	1-1
Morton	0-1	3-1
Motherwell	1-0	3-1
Partick Thistle	1-1	1-1
St Johnstone	2-1	1-0
St Mirren	1-0	7-0
Third Lanark	5-0	1-0

A-Z OF RANGERS

The Ibrox anthology, presented alphabetically

A Along with Dundee United, Aberdeen were half of the New Firm that broke Glasgow's monopoly in the 1970s and 1980s. Former Ranger Alex Ferguson was their manager, while players to have featured for both clubs in recent years include defenders David Robertson and Stephen Wright.

B The name of Berwick Rangers will always fill Rangers fans with dread after their 1-0 SFA Cup win in 1967, masterminded by future Ibrox manager Jock Wallace.

C Closed Circuit TV was thought to be the answer to the number of people trying to see Rangers play Leeds in the 1968 UEFA Cup. Over 43,000 attended, top ticket price being £1.

D The Wee Blue Devil was Alan Morton, who gained the nickname while one of the five forwards (all under five feet seven inches) who tormented England at Wembley in 1928.

E The English invasion happened when Souness took the Ibrox helm. His recruitment drive brought successes – Hateley, Steven and Spackman – and others like Neil Woods and Chris Vinnicombe who played just a handful of games.

F Unlikely as it seems, Rangers once used to compete in the English FA Cup – and in 1887 all but made it to the Final.

They were beaten 3-1 by Aston Villa, who went on to beat West Brom and clinch the trophy, and shortly afterwards were forbidden by the SFA to venture south of the border again.

G Glasgow became Gazza-gow in 1995 when the wayward midfielder signed from Lazio. He's had his ups and downs since then, including two reprimands for 'playing the flute' during Old Firm matches and several sendings-off, but he's also stated he wants to end his career at Ibrox.

H Hardmen come in all shapes and sizes – and Terry Hurlock was undoubtedly one of the toughest Ibrox ever saw. A combative player after Graeme Souness's heart, he arrived from Southampton in 1990 and departed a season later. He established a rugged reputation with his take-no-prisoners approach and became the Premier's most booked player.

I Ibrox internationals are numerous, and include some interesting anomalies. Among these are Richard Gough, a Scot through and through but born in Stockholm, and Andy Goram, likewise a Scots international but born in Lancashire.

J Until the 1997-98 season, St Johnstone had never beaten Rangers in a Premier League game. The clubs' third League clash of the campaign, in January 1998, brought the Saints a 2-0 win.

K Kilmarnock have done rather better, winning one and drawing one of four Premier League meetings in 1996-97. Even so, their record defeat, 8-0, was against Rangers in 1937.

L In 1992 Rangers fought out the unofficial Championship of Great Britain with English Champions Leeds United. Over the two legs of the European Cup Second Round it was the Gers who came out on top.

MLong-serving defender Davie Meiklejohn made 635 competitive appearances for Rangers between 1919 and 1936, playing 15 times for his country. Nicknamed 'Meek', he later managed Partick Thistle.

NIn 1970, 16 of the Rangers first-team squad had surnames ending with the letter 'n'. An alphabetical clean sweep in first-team terms, from keeper Martin to outside-left Persson, was prevented only by ever-present captain John Greig...

OO is the shape most people's mouths make as they survey the magnificence of the current Ibrox filled to capacity.

PThe post of player-manager at Ibrox was inaugurated by Graeme Souness, but would not be continued with after he hung up his boots.

QQueen's Park were the dominant team of the amateur era whose position was usurped by Rangers and their neighbours as professionalism changed the face of Scottish football. Their ground, Hampden Park, has since become something of a second home for the Blues.

RRangers Reserves have often included some very big names over the years as a surfeit of talent has forced some gifted performers to take a turn in the 'stiffs'.

S'And Smith must score' is the most famous soundbite after 'They think it's all over' – and, sadly, it commemorates former Rangers striker Gordon Smith who, after being transferred to Brighton, failed to finish off Manchester United in the 1983 FA Cup Final. The Red Devils triumphed in the replay.

TThe Treble of League, FA Cup and League Cup is a clean sweep of Scottish honours and has been achieved by Rangers five times – first in 1948-49 and most recently in 1992-93.

U Utility players are currently out of favour, but Derek Johnstone was one of the best. He won Cup medals in four different positions – but can't beat Scot Symon, who played from the kick-off in 1942 against Clyde as emergency keeper.

V Maltese team Valletta have twice proved easy meat for Rangers when they've been drawn together in Europe. 1983's Cup Winners' Cup clash ended 18-0 while seven years later a European Cup meeting gave a 10-0 scoreline.

W Though he stayed less than three seasons at Ibrox after signing from Paris Saint Germain, Ray 'Butch' Wilkins made a huge impression with his matchwinning midfield skills.

X When it comes to X-certificate matches you can't beat the Scottish FA Cup Final replay of 1909. It was events after the final whistle which caused the game to go down in history as the 'Hampden Riot'. Such was the unrest from both sets of fans when the anticipated extra time did not materialise that they invaded the pitch. The SFA witheld the Cup and paid compensation to ground owners Queen's Park.

Y Youth has often been given its head in a Rangers shirt over the years. 16-year-old Derek Johnstone won the League Cup in 1971 with the game's only goal, while 1960s winger Willie Henderson became the youngest player bar Denis Law to play internationally for Scotland at 18 years and 269 days.

Z With forwards like McCoist, Durie and Negri around, a Zero on the scoresheet has been a rare occurrence in the 1990s. Rangers failed to score in the League only seven times in 1990-91, six times the following season and four times in 1992-93 – all, needless to say, Championship campaigns.

THROUGH THE YEARS
SEPTEMBER

1939
September
2

When war breaks out, unbeaten Rangers find themselves on top of the Scottish League with five matches played. The competition is abandoned, but the boys in blue go on to dominate what football there was for the next six years.

1941
September
29

The lowest crowd in modern times for a Rangers v Celtic game is recorded today when only 15,000 saw a Glasgow Cup tie end 3-2 to the Blues. There had been trouble at the previous match and admission was by ticket only.

1942
September
11

John Greig, an Ibrox legend as a player if not a manager, is born in Edinburgh. A one-club man, he played 496 League games in blue before moving upstairs and later became the club's public relations supremo.

1987

September

An astounding eight matches played this month, two in the League Cup, result in seven Rangers wins and just a single-goal defeat. This is in the European Cup against Dynamo Kiev, who are beaten 2-0 when they come to Ibrox through goals by Falco and McCoist.

1995

September

30

Paul Gascoigne registers his first League goal for Rangers – and typically chooses the biggest game in Scottish football, the Old Firm derby, in which to do so. His strike confirms Rangers' 2-0 win after Alex Cleland puts their noses in front at Parkhead. Definitely no flute-playing this time…

1996

September

28

Rangers complete two 100 per cent months with a 2-0 win over Celtic at Ibrox. Seven victories in as many games have set them off on the perfect start to a ninth Championship season, equalling the record set by their rivals – and 50,124 fans were there to witness the feat.

BOGEY TEAMS

Any club that plays against Rangers – even if it's four times in a season – is sure to regard the fixture as their own personal Cup Final.

No surprise, then, to find that despite their decade-long domination of Scottish football, Glasgow Rangers have slipped up on a number of occasions against clubs they should by rights wipe the floor with. That said, having the chances to get their revenge and prove that there's no substitute for class means that over the course of a season the cream will float to the top...

When it comes to bogey teams, it's hard to look past the name of Berwick Rangers whose shock 1–0 Cup win in 1967 gets a mention elsewhere in this book. Yet when the fixture was repeated in 1978 the result was a 4–2 victory for the visitors, so we'll regard this as a once in a lifetime freak.

Top of the list of regular problem opponents must be Aberdeen, who inflicted Rangers' first and only five-goal thrashing since the Premier League was established. That January 1985 win was preceded by the two next heaviest losses, 4–0 in 1977 and 1982 respectively. There have also been a trio of embarrassingly emphatic defeats at Ibrox to the same opposition in 1978, 1985 and 1989. Little wonder they're the team Rangers least like to face – indeed the Dons are the only team who have got into double figures against Rangers in a Premier League season. That's happened twice, in 1977–78 and 1981–82.

On the other hand, the team they have the best record against is tiny Glasgow neighbours Hamilton who, in their two Premier League seasons have lost each and every game against Rangers, scoring just two goals and conceding 17. Yet they gave Graeme Souness a red face in 1987 when, in his first full season as manager, they knocked out his side in the first round of the FA Cup, albeit by a single goal. The fact that it spoiled the possibility of a Treble when the end of the season arrived didn't help matters...

Celtic, of course, have always provided stiff opposition and results in those matches have rarely if ever owed anything to current form. As revealed elsewhere, honours in Cup terms are relatively even, with Rangers having the edge in the League.

Europe has seen Rangers bow out to clearly inferior opposition – far too many times in recent history, but to count these as bogey teams when they're rarely faced more than twice might be clouding the issue. Certainly, though, it's recent early-round defeats to the likes of IFK Gothenberg (1997), Levski Sofia (1993) and Sparta Prague (1991) that have been the biggest blots on Walter Smith's otherwise outstanding managerial record.

Domestically, Kilmarnock have had their moments when playing Rangers, while Raith Rovers' Starks Park is never the most inviting of venues. Dundee United have traditionally been tough opponents, having amassed 17 League wins to Rangers' 42 (to end 1996–97 season). Yet it's true to say that Rangers' worst enemy is probably themselves – for on their day no one can stand against them!

LEAGUE RECORD

The Cups may have the glamour – but League success has always been uppermost in Ibrox minds.

Season	Division	P	W	D	L	F-A	Pts	Pos
1890-91	One	18	13	3	2	58-25	29	1=
⭐	Division One Champions							⭐
1891-92	One	22	11	2	9	59-46	24	5th
1892-93	One	18	12	4	2	41-27	28	2nd
1893-94	One	18	8	4	6	44-30	20	4th
1894-95	One	18	10	2	6	41-26	22	3rd
1895-96	One	18	11	4	3	57-39	26	2nd
1896-97	One	18	11	3	4	64-30	25	3rd
1897-98	One	18	13	3	2	71-15	29	2nd
1898-99	One	18	18	—	—	79-18	36	1st
⭐	Division One Champions							⭐
1899-1900	One	18	15	2	1	69-27	32	1st
⭐	Division One Champions							⭐
1900-01	One	20	17	1	2	60-25	35	1st
⭐	Division One Champions							⭐
1901-02	One	18	13	2	3	43-29	28	1st
⭐	Division One Champions							⭐
1902-03	One	22	12	5	5	56-30	29	3rd
1903-04	One	26	16	6	4	80-33	38	4th
1904-05	One	26	19	3	4	83-28	41	2nd

Season	Division	P	W	D	L	F-A	Pts	Pos
1905–06	One	30	15	7	8	58–48	37	4th
1906–07	One	34	19	7	8	69–33	45	3rd
1907–08	One	34	21	8	5	74–40	50	3rd
1908–09	One	34	19	7	8	91–38	45	4th
1909–10	One	34	20	6	8	70–35	46	3rd
1910–11	One	34	23	6	5	90–34	52	1st

⭐ **Division One Champions** ⭐

Season	Division	P	W	D	L	F-A	Pts	Pos
1911–12	One	34	24	3	7	86–34	51	1st

⭐ **Division One Champions** ⭐

Season	Division	P	W	D	L	F-A	Pts	Pos
1912–13	One	34	24	5	5	76–41	53	1st

⭐ **Division One Champions** ⭐

Season	Division	P	W	D	L	F-A	Pts	Pos
1913–14	One	38	27	5	6	79–31	59	2nd
1914–15	One	38	23	4	11	74–47	50	3rd
1915–16	One	38	25	6	7	87–39	56	2nd
1916–17	One	38	24	5	9	68–32	53	3rd
1917–18	One	34	25	6	3	66–24	56	1st

⭐ **Division One Champions** ⭐

Season	Division	P	W	D	L	F-A	Pts	Pos
1918–19	One	34	26	5	3	86–16	57	2nd
1919–20	One	42	31	9	2	106–25	71	1st

⭐ **Division One Champions** ⭐

Season	Division	P	W	D	L	F-A	Pts	Pos
1920–21	One	42	35	6	1	91–24	76	1st

⭐ **Division One Champions** ⭐

Season	Division	P	W	D	L	F-A	Pts	Pos
1921–22	One	42	28	10	4	83–26	66	2nd
1922–23	One	38	23	9	6	67–29	55	1st

⭐ **Division One Champions** ⭐

Season	Division	P	W	D	L	F-A	Pts	Pos
1923–24	One	38	25	9	4	72–22	59	1st

⭐ **Division One Champions** ⭐

Season	Division	P	W	D	L	F-A	Pts	Pos
1924–25	One	38	25	10	3	76–26	60	1st
⭐ Division One Champions ⭐								
1925–26	One	38	19	6	13	79–55	44	6th
1926–27	One	38	23	10	5	85–41	56	1st
⭐ Division One Champions ⭐								
1927–28	One	38	26	8	4	109–36	60	1st
⭐ Division One Champions ⭐								
1928–29	One	38	30	7	1	107–32	67	1st
⭐ Division One Champions ⭐								
1929–30	One	38	28	4	6	94–32	60	1st
⭐ Division One Champions ⭐								
1930–31	One	38	27	6	5	96–29	60	1st
⭐ Division One Champions ⭐								
1931–32	One	38	28	5	5	118–42	61	2nd
1932–33	One	38	26	10	2	113–43	62	1st
⭐ Division One Champions ⭐								
1933–34	One	38	30	6	2	118–41	66	1st
⭐ Division One Champions ⭐								
1934–35	One	38	25	5	8	96–46	55	1st
⭐ Division One Champions ⭐								
1935–36	One	38	27	7	4	110–43	61	2nd
1936–37	One	38	26	9	3	88–32	61	1st
⭐ Division One Champions ⭐								
1937–38	One	38	18	13	7	75–49	49	3rd

RANGERS

Season	Division	P	W	D	L	F-A	Pts	Pos
1938–39	One	38	25	9	4	112–55	59	1st

⭐ **Division One Champions** ⭐

Season	Division	P	W	D	L	F-A	Pts	Pos
1946–47	A	30	21	4	5	76–26	46	1st

⭐ **Division A Champions** ⭐

Season	Division	P	W	D	L	F-A	Pts	Pos
1947–48	A	30	21	4	5	64–28	46	2nd
1948–49	A	30	20	6	4	63–32	46	1st

⭐ **Division A Champions** ⭐

Season	Division	P	W	D	L	F-A	Pts	Pos
1949–50	A	30	22	6	2	58–26	50	1st

⭐ **Division A Champions** ⭐

Season	Division	P	W	D	L	F-A	Pts	Pos
1950–51	A	30	17	4	9	64–37	38	2nd
1951–52	A	30	16	9	5	61–31	41	2nd
1952–53	A	30	18	7	5	80–39	43	1st

⭐ **Division A Champions** ⭐

Season	Division	P	W	D	L	F-A	Pts	Pos
1953–54	A	30	13	8	9	56–35	34	4th
1954–55	A	30	19	3	8	67–33	41	3rd
1955–56	A	34	22	8	4	85–27	52	1st

⭐ **Division A Champions** ⭐

Season	Division	P	W	D	L	F-A	Pts	Pos
1956–57	One	34	26	3	5	96–48	55	1st

⭐ **Division One Champions** ⭐

Season	Division	P	W	D	L	F-A	Pts	Pos
1957–58	One	34	22	5	7	89–49	49	1st

⭐ **Division One Champions** ⭐

Season	Division	P	W	D	L	F-A	Pts	Pos
1958–59	One	34	21	8	5	92–51	50	1st

⭐ **Division One Champions** ⭐

Season	Division	P	W	D	L	F-A	Pts	Pos
1959–60	One	34	17	8	9	72–38	42	3rd

RANGERS

Season	Division	P	W	D	L	F-A	Pts	Pos
1960–61	One	34	23	5	6	88-46	51	1st
★ Division One Champions ★								
1961–62	One	34	22	7	5	84-31	51	2nd
1962–63	One	34	25	7	2	94-28	57	1st
★ Division One Champions ★								
1963–64	One	34	25	5	4	85-31	55	1st
★ Division One Champions ★								
1964–65	One	34	18	8	8	78-35	44	5th
1965–66	One	34	25	5	4	91-29	55	2nd
1966–67	One	34	24	7	3	92-31	55	2nd
1967–68	One	34	28	5	1	93-34	61	2nd
1968–69	One	34	21	7	6	81-32	49	2nd
1969–70	One	34	19	7	8	67-40	45	2nd
1970–71	One	34	16	9	9	58-34	41	4th
1971–72	One	34	21	2	11	71-38	44	3rd
1972–73	One	34	26	4	4	74-30	56	2nd
1973–74	One	34	21	6	7	67-34	48	3rd
1974–75	One	34	25	6	3	86-33	56	1st
★ Division One Champions ★								
1975–76	Premier	36	23	8	5	60-24	54	1st
★ Premier Division Champions ★								
1976–77	Premier	36	18	10	8	62-37	46	2nd
1977–78	Premier	36	24	7	5	76-39	55	1st
★ Premier Division Champions ★								
1978–79	Premier	36	18	9	9	52-35	45	2nd
1979–80	Premier	36	15	7	14	50-46	37	5th
1980–81	Premier	36	16	12	8	60-32	44	3rd
1981–82	Premier	36	16	11	9	57-45	43	3rd

Season	Division	P	W	D	L	F-A	Pts	Pos
1982–83	Premier	36	13	12	11	52-41	38	4th
1983–84	Premier	36	15	12	9	53-41	42	4th
1984–85	Premier	36	13	12	11	47-38	38	4th
1985–86	Premier	36	13	9	14	53-45	35	5th
1986–87	Premier	44	31	7	6	85-23	69	1st

⭐ **Premier Division Champions** ⭐

Season	Division	P	W	D	L	F-A	Pts	Pos
1987–88	Premier	44	26	8	10	85-34	60	3rd
1988–89	Premier	36	26	4	6	62-26	56	1st

⭐ **Premier Division Champions** ⭐

Season	Division	P	W	D	L	F-A	Pts	Pos
1989–90	Premier	36	20	11	5	48-19	51	1st

⭐ **Premier Division Champions** ⭐

Season	Division	P	W	D	L	F-A	Pts	Pos
1990–91	Premier	36	24	7	5	62-23	53	1st

⭐ **Premier Division Champions** ⭐

Season	Division	P	W	D	L	F-A	Pts	Pos
1991–92	Premier	44	33	6	5	101-31	72	1st

⭐ **Premier Division Champions** ⭐

Season	Division	P	W	D	L	F-A	Pts	Pos
1992–93	Premier	44	33	7	4	97-35	73	1st

⭐ **Premier Division Champions** ⭐

Season	Division	P	W	D	L	F-A	Pts	Pos
1993–94	Premier	44	22	14	8	74-41	58	1st

⭐ **Premier Division Champions** ⭐

Season	Division	P	W	D	L	F-A	Pts	Pos
1994–95	Premier	36	20	9	7	60-35	69	1st

⭐ **Premier Division Champions** ⭐

Season	Division	P	W	D	L	F-A	Pts	Pos
1995–96	Premier	36	27	6	3	85-25	87	1st

⭐ **Premier Division Champions** ⭐

Season	Division	P	W	D	L	F-A	Pts	Pos
1996–97	Premier	36	25	5	6	85-33	80	1st

⭐ **Premier Division Champions** ⭐

THROUGH THE YEARS
OCTOBER

1874
October
12

Rangers play their first ever Scottish Cup tie, beating Oxford 2–0 at Queen's Park Recreation Ground. They could have made their debut the previous term but had been late in applying for membership of the Scottish FA.

1946
October
8

Centre-half Colin Jackson is born in London. A one-club man, he registered 343 League appearances in a blue shirt but, though a regular choice, missed the 1972 Cup Winners' Cup Final through injury.

1964
October
27

The season having got off to a bad start, with just two wins in eight games, the goal block was smashed today with a 7–0 win against the minnows of St Mirren. Next game saw Rangers smash six past Clyde.

1966
October

Rangers played three matches at Hampden Park in less than two weeks. The League Cup Semi-Final with Aberdeen was drawn 2-2, a replay ended 2-0 to Rangers but the Final against Celtic was lost by a single goal.

1987
October
17

An infamous Old Firm clash that ended 2-2 saw Rangers keeper Chris Woods ordered off in an acrimonious scene. Defender Graham Roberts took over in goal, but incensed the Celtic fans as he turned towards the Ibrox support and appeared to conduct their chants. That landed him in court with Woods, Terry Butcher and Celtic's Frank McAvennie, although the case against him was found not proven. Despite an end-of-season move to Chelsea, Roberts would retain an affection for the club.

1988
October
8

Ian Durrant suffered serious knee ligament injuries in a tackle with Aberdeen's Neil Simpson, an incident that seriously hampered his progress. He recaptured his form in the 1992-93 season but sadly failed to fulfil potential thereafter.

KEEPERS KORNER

They may not wear the world-famous blue – but Rangers keepers have played a big part in laying the foundations for success. Here are just a few of the biggest names.

 ## JERRY DAWSON

Rangers keepers have tended to hang around a bit – but Jerry Dawson's stickability takes some beating. Until surpassed by Peter McCloy, the 545 appearances he made between 1929 and 1945 remained a record.

To stay in first-team contention for the best part of two decades takes some doing, and when Dawson replaced the acclaimed Tom Hamilton for the first time in August 1930 he was on the way to a place in the record books. The pair battled for the Number 1 jersey of the next two seasons, but the younger man won through and would see out the decade as undisputed first choice.

Dawson was a happy-go-lucky character who made friends on and off the pitch. Interestingly his real christian name was James, but a Burnley keeper with the same surname had played for England and his team-mates gave Dawson (born in Falkirk in 1909) the more familiar appellation.

He played all through wartime football until breaking a leg against Hibernian at Hampden Park in 1944. The injury threatened his footballing future, but he came back to play in the 2-2 friendly against Moscow Dynamo the following year, signing off with a flourish before spending the last four years of his Scottish League career with his home-town club.

Dawson won five Championships, two SFA Cups and sundry wartime honours while between the posts at Ibrox. Dependable rather that eye-catching, his style was one that found success at international level too – 14 caps were obtained pre-war, plus more in wartime internationals, and many mourned when he died in 1977.

JERRY DAWSON RANGERS APPS 1929-45				
League	FA Cup	League Cup	Europe	Total
236	30	—	—	266

PETER McCLOY

Peter McCloy is the longest-serving goalkeeper ever to play for Rangers, having amassed over 500 appearances for the club between 1970 and 1978. During this period he kept a respectable 200 clean sheets – not surprising when you consider the fact that he was six foot four inches, a height which towered above his contemporaries.

His nickname, the 'Girvan Lighthouse', came from the place on the Ayrshire coast where he was born on 16 November 1946. Peter followed in the footsteps of his father, who had played in goal for St Mirren, and began his professional career with Motherwell. He joined the club in 1970, but conceded two goals in his first game as Rangers lost 2-1 to Dunfermline.

McCloy played at a time when there were great Scottish keepers in abundance and the international green jersey was fiercely contested between the likes of Bobby Clark, David Harvey and Alan Rough. It's largely because of this that he only managed four caps for his country, although he enjoyed considerably more success at his club.

His skill in goal is illustrated by the number of quality players that challenged his Number 1 position. During his time at Rangers he saw off the likes of Stewart Kennedy and Jim Stewart and made the position his own for 16 years. He was eventually replaced by England international Chris Woods, which was no shame considering that Peter was 40 years old by this time.

His honours while playing for Rangers give testament to his services to the club and included one League Championship, four Scottish Cups, four League Cups and the European Cup Winners' Cup in 1972.

Although he will always be remembered for the goals that he saved, a thought should also be spared for all those that he set up. The distance that McCloy could gain with his clearances were renowned, and there were several instances when a goal resulted directly from one of these monster boots downfield. After retiring, he returned to Ayrshire where he runs a hotel and is involved with junior football: his son Stephen also went into the professional game.

PETER McCLOY RANGERS APPS 1970–86				
League	FA Cup	League Cup	Europe	Total
351	55	86	43	535

CHRIS WOODS

A spectacular yet reliable keeper, this popular Englishman impressed many during his 200–plus games for Rangers and proved £600,000 well spent. The England international was Graeme Souness' second big-name signing after Terry Butcher in the Ibrox revolution of 1986. He was an extremely capable goalkeeper who enjoyed a highly successful career at both club and international level.

Though he never played a League game for first club Nottingham Forest, Woods was a member of the side that won the 1978 League Cup after Peter Shilton fell injured. He went on to clock up nearly 200 League appearances for QPR and Norwich City, and came to the attention of his national team when on 16 June 1985 he made the first of 43 appearances, on this occasion against the USA.

Woods's first season at Ibrox saw him help his side to the League Cup and Premier League title. There's no denying he benefited from playing behind a defence of Butcher and Richard Gough, but few forwards managed to beat him when they eluded those two giants.

Ironically it would take until 1990-91, his last season with Rangers, for Woods to register an ever-present campaign and his 48 games in League, domestic Cups and European Cup saw him keep 27 clean sheets. That period would also be his most successful with England to that date, winning eight caps under the management of Graham Taylor.

When Walter Smith took over from Souness, Woods quickly made way for Andy Goram, the limit on non-nationals in European competition causing headaches. After four successful seasons with Sheffield Wednesday, he had joined the US Soccer Federation, but ex-Ibrox boss Souness brought him back to Britain in 1996 when he signed him for

Southampton. Sadly Woods broke his leg within weeks of his arrival at the Dell and his top-flight career was over.

CHRIS WOODS RANGERS APPS 1986-91				
League	FA Cup	League Cup	Europe	Total
173	15	21	21	230

 # ANDY GORAM

Since his arrival at Ibrox in 1991, the commanding presence of Andy Goram has been crucial to Rangers as they continued to dominate the Scottish scene. A much-publicised fall-out with Walter Smith in 1995 led to his transfer-listing, but there was never any real danger he would go, and the kick up the backside ulitmately proved beneficial.

The shot-stopper born in Bury, 13 April 1964, of Scottish parents, began his career with nearby Oldham Athletic, for whom he signed in 1981 as a teenager and stayed to play 195 League games until moving to Hibernian in 1987. He was already a Scotland international by this time, having made his debut on 16 October 1985 v East Germany.

Goram was superb in his four years in Edinburgh, increasing his international honours if not domestic silverware, and it was no surprise when his reliability was recognised at Ibrox and he was persuaded by Walter Smith to join Rangers in 1991 as Chris Woods' replacement. Although far from tall by goalkeeping standards at five foot 11 inches, his safe handling and speed around the box have proved crucial, especially in one-on-one situations. Many a forward has been thwarted by his bursts from the line to block goalbound shots.

His first season at Ibrox saw him ever-present in League and Cups, registering 55 appearances in total and 26 shut-outs as the club powered to four in a row.

Goram is also a cricket international and has represented Scotland on many occasions. As he approaches 200 League games for Rangers, having exceeded a career total of 500, he remains in his prime in goalkeeping terms. Whether or not Walter Smith's successor looks for new blood, there's plenty of life in him yet.

ANDY GORAM RANGERS APPS 1991–(97)				
League	FA Cup	League Cup	Europe	Total
184	21	22	30	257

BEST SEASON 3

While the previous season had seen the arrival of big names like Gascoigne, Wright and Petric, 1996–97 was the year it all really gelled together – and more importantly for Rangers fans when the Old Firm rivalry reached level pegging. This, of course, was Rangers' ninth Championship in a row, equalling the haul of Jock Stein's classic Celtic team. The stage was set...

While the FA Cup had been taken the previous term, it was the Coca-Cola Cup that this time round would be added to the trophy cabinet. How comforting it was to have a piece of silverware under your belt before Christmas – yet anyone who thought Hearts would be easy meat in the Final was sadly mistaken! Having brushed aside Clydebank, Ayr, Hibs and Dunfermline on a 16–2 aggregate, the Final nearly saw an upset: Rangers pulled through 4–3, a brace apiece from McCoist and Gascoigne.

No FA Cup run this year, losing out to Celtic at Parkhead. But in all other departments they showed themselves streets ahead of the competition from across the city, all four Glasgow derbies in the League going to the blue side. Yet the Gers had entered October with a 100 per cent record of seven wins out of seven, piling in the goals from all quarters. Dutchman Peter Van Vossen and German full-back Jorg Albertz both contributed alongside the multi-national likes of Gazza, Laudrup and Erik Bo Andersen.

December saw 22 goals achieved in just seven games, and, in all honesty, the Championship was beginning to look a cakewalk even then. No one seemed likely to threaten pole position until March, when two defeats in a month for the first time – both at home, against Dundee United and Kilmarnock – gave the chasing pack hope. That hope was quickly and cruelly killed off in April, two games against Dunfermline and Raith seeing ten goals rain in without reply.

Amazingly, two more defeats came in May when the title had been mathematically secured and Rangers took their foot off the gas, but enough had already been seen to know that this was a side that would take some stopping in the search for an historic tenth title. The sick list was sometimes so long that in March Walter Smith had to bring back Hateley and summon up Andy Dibble from Manchester City reserves to fill in for injured keeper Andy Goram.

1996–97 LEAGUE RECORD

Opponents	Home	Away
Aberdeen	2-2	3-0
Aberdeen	4-0	2-2
Celtic	2-0	1-0
Celtic	3-1	1-0
Dundee United	1-0	0-1
Dundee United	0-2	1-0
Dunfermline A	3-1	5-2
Dunfermline A	4-0	3-0
Hearts	3-0	4-1
Hearts	0-0	1-3
Hibernian	4-3	1-2
Hibernian	3-1	2-1
Kilmarnock	4-2	4-1
Kilmarnock	1-2	1-1
Motherwell	5-0	1-0
Motherwell	0-2	3-1
Raith Rovers	1-0	2-2
Raith Rovers	4-0	6-0

THROUGH THE YEARS
NOVEMBER

1915
November
20

Ending a game with less than 11 men is sadly far from unknown – but for the first and last time ever Rangers started with only nine, the other two plus a reserve having missed their connection due to the infamous Glasgow fog! Eleven-man Falkirk took full advantage, and it was a surprise the score was kept down to 2-0.

1981
November
28

Goals by Cooper and Redford bring John Greig a welcome piece of silverware – the Scottish League Cup, thanks to a win againt Dundee United at Hampden. It would prove the only success of a disappointing season in which Rangers could only finish third in the League and lost the FA Cup Final to a rampant Aberdeen, managed by ex-Ranger Alex Ferguson.

1988

November

All change in the Ibrox boardroom as millionaire fan David Murray takes control. The changes he's wrought in the team and the stadium can clearly be seen today.

1989

November

25

Ray Wilkins earns a standing Ibrox ovation for his performance against Dunfermline in his final game for Rangers before leaving to join QPR.

1994

November

13

Ally McCoist is given the freedom of East Kilbride, his home borough – and announces he and wife Allison are expecting their first child.

GREAT DEFENDERS

**They may not hog the headlines,
but Rangers defenders have played
a major part in keeping the club at the
very top of Scottish and world football.
Try these giants for size...**

 ## RON McKINNON

Born in Glasgow on 20 August 1940, Ron McKinnon played youth football before being signed by Rangers in 1959, intially as a midfielder. Switching to centre-half to cover for a spate of injuries, he found this was his best position and he became not only one of the the the best central defenders ever to play for Rangers but played 28 full internationals for Scotland. Celtic's better-known Billy McNeill battled McKinnon head-on for the Number 5 shirt, only winning one more cap.

Rangers, under Scot Symon's stewardship, built on their rock-solid defence and were soon challenging Celtic for mastery of Scotland. The League and Scottish Cup Double in 1962-63 was followed by the Treble the following year: two more Scottish Cups and two League Cups would be added to

McKinnon's victory roll during his Ibrox career. He was a defender when defenders were ordered never to cross the halfway line, and goals were as rare as hen's teeth: the first League strike to his name came on the last day of 1966. He nevertheless remained a bastion of the defence.

He would have been an automatic choice for the side that won the European Cup Winners' Cup in 1972, but had broken his leg earlier in the competition against Sporting Lisbon – an injury that ultimately called time on his Rangers career. Colin Jackson and then Derek Johnstone both laid claim to the Number 5 shirt, the latter switching successfully from a striking role. Having failed to play his way back into first-team contention, the end of the 1972–73 season saw McKinnon move abroad to South Africa and then on to Australia. Those who saw him at his peak would name him as a member of Rangers' best–ever backline.

RON McKINNON RANGERS RECORD 1959-73									
League		FA Cup		League Cup		Europe		Total	
Apps	Goals	Apps	Goals	Apps	Goals	Apps	Goals	Apps	Goals
301	2	44	—	83	—	45	1	473	3

SANDY JARDINE

Sandy Jardine had the skill, strength, and pace needed to play in almost any position Rangers required of him. This, coupled with his calm temperament and his reputation as a fair player, meant he was destined to become one of the great players not only of his generation but of all-time.

William Pullar Jardine, to give him his full name, was born in Edinburgh on 31 December 1948 and lived and played football there until he was signed by Rangers at the age of 18.

Ironically, his debut was against home-town club Hearts but right-half Jardine and team-mates showed little mercy as Rangers brushed them aside 5-1. After playing in midfield, on the wings and at centre-forward he eventually established himself at full-back, playing on left or right with equal ease.

Jardine proved invaluable and was part of the Treble-winning squads of 1975-76 and 1977-78. These honours contributed to his impressive haul of three Championship medals, five Scottish Cup medals and five League Cup medals amassed during his time at Ibrox. In addition, he was also part of the Rangers team that triumphed in the European Cup Winners' Cup of 1972. Despite this success at club level, Sandy's quality shone when he took to the field as full-back for his country, as he did on 38 occasions.

Jardine left Rangers in 1982 and returned to his home city of Edinburgh to play for Hearts. He helped them to promotion and provided them with excellent service, both on and off the field, playing on into his late thirties as he became assistant manager and eventually joint manager with Alex MacDonald in 1987. He hung up his boots at that point, but mysteriously carried the can in 1988 for a run of poor results, MacDonald retaining his post. Nevertheless Jardine, with over 1,000 top-class appearances to his credit, and twice voted Scotland's Footballer of the Year, retains a special place in the affections of two of Scotland's footballing cities.

SANDY JARDINE RANGERS RECORD 1967-82									
League		FA Cup		League Cup		Europe		Total	
Apps	Goals	Apps	Goals	Apps	Goals	Apps	Goals	Apps	Goals
451	42	64	8	107	25	52	2	674	77

COLIN JACKSON

Born in London on 8 October 1946, Colin Jackson remains one of the few players to have been born outside Scotland and still represent them at international level, having been capped eight times. He moved to Rangers in 1963 from Sunnybank Athletic, a small team from Aberdeen and stayed with the club until 1982.

Despite his reputation as a strong, reliable defender, Jackson did score for Rangers on occasion. Of these, none could have been as important as his winning goal in the last minute against Aberdeen in the League Cup Final in 1979. There is little doubt that it was the finest moment in his career. He played the first of his 43 Old Firm games in August 1968's 2-0 League Cup defeat at Ibrox.

Although Colin often found himself on the substitute's bench, his dedication to the club was unquestionable and he rightly collected many honours during his years of service. As well as three League Championships and three Scottish Cups, he also received six League Cup medals.

But the most bitter-sweet medal he received must surely be from the European Cup Winners' Cup in 1972. Jackson had been a key figure in the side which had fought its way to the final in Barcelona, only to be denied a place through injury as he failed a fitness test shortly before the game. It was small consolation that he watched his team triumph and was given a winner's medal. Colin Jackson retains his connections with Ibrox today by assisting as a matchday host.

COLIN JACKSON RANGERS RECORD 1968-82									
League		FA Cup		League Cup		Europe		Total	
Apps	Goals	Apps	Goals	Apps	Goals	Apps	Goals	Apps	Goals
334	23	53	8	75	8	35	1	497	40

RICHARD GOUGH

Big-spending Rangers could have saved themselves £1 million had they signed up a teenage Richard Gough rather than waiting for him to make a name for himself. Globetrotting Gough, who was born in Stockholm in 1962 of Swedish/Scottish parentage, was brought up in South Africa, but on returning to Scotland was seen but rejected by a club for whom he would one day prove one of the most successful skippers ever.

Rangers' temporary loss was Dundee United's gain, and his six years in orange ended with a big-money move to Tottenham Hotspur. His boss at Tannadice had refused to let him go to Ibrox, believing there would be an outcry. But six months after appearing in the English FA Cup Final Gough was back north of the border, playing alongside Terry Butcher as Graeme Souness's team swept all before it.

The reasoning behind Gough's departure from Spurs – at £1.5 million, twice his original pricetag – was that his family had not settled in England. Yet his leadership had been an important part of the drive to Wembley, and it was clear by October 1987, when he signed for Graeme Souness, that the one and a half seasons spent south of the border had turned him into not only an all-round player but an inspirational skipper.

If he had missed out on the FA Cup, that was nothing to get too upset about: his time at Ibrox would bring 18 trophies, making Gough the most successful Rangers captain ever. He'd made his international debut in 1983 while with Dundee United and proceeded to duplicate his domestic success on that bigger stage. Despite a premature end to his Scotland career after just 61 caps – a difference of opinion with national coach Andy Roxburgh after a humiliating World Cup loss to

RANGERS

Portugal – he seemed to be even more effective playing for his club thereafter.

Such was Gough's influence at Ibrox that, after making the decision to play out his career in the US soccer league with Kansas City, he was sensationally released to rejoin Rangers as their bid to make it ten Championships in a row seemed likely to founder. It goes without saying that fortunes took an upturn, and he slotted in as if he'd never been away.

RICHARD GOUGH RANGERS RECORD 1988–(97)									
League		FA Cup		League Cup		Europe		Total	
Apps	Goals	Apps	Goals	Apps	Goals	Apps	Goals	Apps	Goals
263	19	29	1	36	3	34	3	362	26

THE WAR YEARS

**During the First World War, English League
football was suspended for the duration
after the 1914–15 season.**

Although the Cup was abandoned north of the border,
the Scottish League carried on, even though there was
inevitable disruption for the leading teams – and the
players' wages were reduced to a maximum of £2 per week.

Celtic dominated the Scottish scene, and it wasn't until
1917–18 that Rangers broke their stranglehold, adding a
Glasgow Cup Double thanks to a 4–1 win over Partick
Thistle. So if wartime football was thought to be good for
morale, no doubt the other side of Glasgow was the more
grateful.

In the Second World War, things were rather different. All
League football was suspended and, though the government
eventually decreed that football was permissable, it was clearly
not possible to organise the game on national lines. Regional
leagues were therefore organised across Britain.

When war broke out, an unbeaten Rangers had been top
of the Scottish League with nine points from five fixtures
(this, of course, in the era of two points for a win). They
might have been disappointed that the competition was
immediately abandoned, but if they were they managed to
turn their frustration into a run of fine form. Out of 34
competitions in which they participated during the course of
hostilities, Rangers won an unbelievable 25.

The club had their share of war heroes, among them Ian
McPherson who took part in the first Royal Air Force

bombing raids on Germany and won the Distinguished Flying Cross, while on the ground Willie Thornton earned the Military Medal for his part in the invasion of Sicily. Other players were able to stay in the area by working in reserved occupations, helping the war effort in local factories or shipyards while continuing to play their football part-time. Crowds were small by comparison

Guest players were able to be drafted in to make up for those Rangers inter-war stars off on active service. Stanley Matthews, perhaps the greatest winger of all time, made two appearances: the first was against Morton in March 1940, while the second, over a year later, was the Glasgow Merchants Charity Cup Final played at Hampden Park in May 1941. Rangers not only beat Partick 3-0, but retained the trophy in 1942, 1944 and 1945.

That match saw Matthews playing alongside future Manchester City manager Les McDowall and former Ranger Torrance 'Torry' Gillick (who'd been transferred to Everton in 1935 for a club record £8,000 fee and would return in 1945). St Johnstone's Willie McIntosh proved the period's sharp-shooter, bagging 60 goals in just 66 games, while future manager Scot Symon was also a regular in the half-back line.

Rangers kept a second string going throughout the war years, and it was indicative of their strength that this reserve team beat the first XIs of many of their opponents. News filtered back from further afield that a team of Rangers-supporting prisoners of war had won the championship played between teams of captured Allied soldiers in Germany!

There was a sadder side to all this, though, for many of the club's supporters and some of the players would not return once hostilities ceased in 1945: many legendary names would no longer be seen on the team sheet in 'official' League games, either through age or infirmity.

THROUGH THE YEARS
DECEMBER

1906
December
8

Left-winger Alex Smith scores Rangers' 1,000th League goal against Clyde, adding another in an emphatic 5–1 win.

1953
December
8

There's often been speculation as to which club is the unofficial champion of Britain, so much pride was at stake when Arsenal arrived at Ibrox to inaugurate new floodlights. The hotly contested friendly ended with a 2–1 win for the Londoners.

1986
December
27

A 2–0 win against Dundee United sparks a 19-game unbeaten run which would see Rangers add the League to the League Cup already secured. It was Graham Roberts' first game in a blue shirt since arriving from Spurs.

1994
December
12

Centre-forward Duncan Ferguson, the so-called 'wild man of Ibrox', is offloaded to Everton for £4.26 million. He still awaits trial on a headbutting charge that would see him spend time behind bars, but nevertheless makes Rangers a profit on his transfer since he leaves before triggering an appearances bonus.

1996
December
17

Speedy Danish striker Erik Bo Andersen bags a three-goal haul against Kilmarnock at Ibrox as Rangers power towards a ninth title. His appearances during the season would be limited by injury, but he still managed to notch nine goals in six appearances, plus a further 11 as substitute.

THE KITBAG

These days it's one of Glasgow's most popular fashion items – but once players would have walked through fire just to wear it. We're talking about the Rangers shirt, and, depending on your age, you may recall many different designs and details as the seasons have passed.

Though the colour of today's shirt is very definitely dark blue, supporters of mature years may recall a lighter hue. Shorts have always been white and socks black, though the red tops dwindled to a stripe in the 1960s and occasionally disappeared altogether.

The away kit was not dissimilar with light blue hoops on white – a pattern often likened to a butcher's traditional striped apron! Blue with red and white hoops replaced it, while a brief flirtation with Real Madrid–style all white in the 1960s dazzled in the newly installed floodlights. Recently the choice of away strip has varied between blue and orange strips and a lighter, violet hue.

When sponsorship arrived in 1984, both Glasgow clubs were sponsored by CR Smith, the idea being to bridge the divide between the clubs' supporters. Since then McEwan's Lager has been the name on those proud chests, the initial ugly typeface giving way to the current classical style.

Talking of styles, today's lightweight item would have been laughed at in days of old when, if you were playing in heavy rain, your shirt would be guaranteed to soak up several pounds of water. The 1950s–style jersey looks more like what we'd now term a rugby shirt, buttoned at the neck and with a flapping collar. The simple white-trimmed v-neck ruled through the 1960s, giving way to a crew-neck of the same colour as the shirt. This was when the badge, of the club initials, made its first appearance on the left breast. The mid 1980s saw a white pin-stripe appear, coincidentally something Liverpool adopted south of the border.

The early 1990s brought a wrapover-style collar with zigzag stitching, courtesy of Admiral, while Umbro who succeeded them gave the shirt a subtle check in the fabric that caught the light quite attractively. A stripe also appeared down the side of the shorts. The badge on the shorts has been a long-running affair which spread to the socks too.

The kit manufacturers are always keen to get their mark on somewhere. The strip has gained a triple stripe around the arms and shorts since the German giants took this on: Umbro, in the 1980s, had a triangle on the right breast to counterbalance the badge on the other side, though the mid 1990s saw the Adidas logo, club crest and sponsor's name centred right down the middle of the shirt. Admiral, who took on kit manufacturing duties between the two, put their nautical-style logo on the right breast too, as well as on the socks.

The 1996-97 season saw the kit become the most colourful perhaps for many years. White fold-over collars to the shirts with a white 'v' under the chin has a blue-red-blue trim, which was reproduced both down the side of the shorts and on two white flashes extending from the shoulders and going halfway down the front of the shirt.

The away kit became white shirts with a red badge (club crest in white) and dark red shorts, a blue-red-blue stripe down the right extending to the shorts. Like the home kit, it featured a yellow Premier League badge on the left arm.

No matter what the shirt looks like, one thing's for sure – competition to wear the real thing has never been stiffer.

EUROPEAN CUP

Glasgow Rangers' ultimate goal – and their record so far.

Stage	Opponents	Home	Away	Agg
1956-57				
Preliminary	Bye			
Round 1	Nice	2-1	1-2	3-3
	Rangers lost the replay 1-3			
1957-58				
Preliminary	St Etienne	3-1	1-2	4-3
Round 1	AC Milan	1-4	0-2	1-6
1959-60				
Qualifier	Anderlecht	5-2	2-0	7-2
Round 1	Red Star Bratislava	4-3	1-1	5-4
Round 2	Sparta Rotterdam	0-1	3-2	3-3
	Rangers won the replay 3-2			
Semi-Final	Eintracht Frankfurt	3-6	1-6	4-12
1961-62				
Preliminary	Monaco	3-2	3-2	6-4
Round 1	Vorwaerts Berlin	4-1	2-1	6-2
Quarter-Final	Standard Liege	2-0	1-4	3-4
1963-64				
Preliminary	Real Madrid	0-1	0-6	0-7
1964-65				
Preliminary	Red Star Belgrade	3-1	2-4	5-5
	Rangers won the replay 3-1			
Round 1	Rapid Vienna	1-0	2-0	3-0
Quarter-Final	Inter Milan	1-0	1-3	2-3

Stage	Opponents	Home	Away	Agg
1975-76				
Round 1	Bohemians	4-1	1-1	5-2
Round 2	St Etienne	1-2	0-2	1-4
1976-77				
Round 1	Zurich	1-1	0-1	1-2
1978-79				
Round 1	Juventus	2-0	0-1	2-1
Round 2	PSV Eindhoven	0-0	3-2	3-2
Quarter-Final	Cologne	1-1	0-1	1-2
1987-88				
Round 1	Dynamo Kiev	2-0	0-1	2-1
Round 2	Gornik Zabrze	3-1	1-1	4-2
Quarter-Final	Steaua Bucharest	2-1	0-2	2-3
1989-90				
Round 1	Bayern Munich	1-3	0-0	1-3
1990-91				
Round 1	Valletta	6-0	4-0	10-0
Round 2	Red Star Belgrade	1-1	0-3	1-4
1991-92				
Round 1	Sparta Prague	2-1	0-1	2-2
	Rangers lost on away goals			
1992-93				
Round 1	Lyngby	2-0	1-0	3-0
Round 2	Leeds United	2-1	2-1	4-2
Group A	Marseille	2-2	—	—
Group A	CSKA Moscow	—	1-0	—
Group A	FC Brugge	—	1-1	—
Group A	FC Brugge	2-1	—	—
Group A	Marseille	—	1-1	—
Group A	CSKA Moscow	0-0	—	—

Rangers failed to qualify for the Quarter-Final

Stage	Opponents	Home	Away	Agg
1993-94				
Round 1	Levski Sofia	3-2	1-2	4-4
	Rangers lost on away goals			
1994-95				
Preliminary	AEK Athens	0-1	0-2	0-3
1995-96				
Preliminary	Anorthosis Famagusta	1-0	0-0	1-0
Group A	Steaua Bucharest	—	0-1	—
Group A	Borussia Dortmund	2-2	—	—
Group A	Juventus	—	1-4	—
Group A	Juventus	0-4	—	—
Group A	Steaua Bucharest	1-1	—	—
Group A	Borussia Dortmund	—	2-2	—
	Rangers failed to qualify for the Quarter-Final			
1996-97				
Preliminary	Vladikavkaz	3-1	7-2	10-3
Group A	Grasshoppers	—	0-3	—
Group A	Auxerre	1-2	—	—
Group A	Ajax	—	1-4	—
Group A	Ajax	0-1	—	—
Group A	Grasshoppers	2-1	—	—
Group A	Auxerre	—	1-2	—
	Rangers failed to qualify for the Quarter-Final			
1997-98				
Qualifier 1	GI Gotu	6-0	5-0	11-0
Qualifier 2	IFK Gothenberg	1-1	0-3	1-4

EUROPEAN CUP WINNERS' CUP

The competition that brought Rangers their first European trophy, plus two further Final appearances.

Stage	Opponents	Home	Away	Agg
1960-61				
Qualifier	Ferencvaros	4-2	1-2	5-4
Quarter-Final	B Moenchengladbach	8-0	3-0	11-0
Semi-Final	Wolves	2-0	1-1	3-1
Final	Fiorentina	0-2	1-2	1-4
1962-63				
Round 1	Seville	4-0	0-2	4-2
Round 2	Tottenham Hotspur	2-3	2-5	4-8
1966-67				
Round 1	Glentoran	4-0	1-1	5-1
Round 2	Borussia Dortmund	2-1	0-0	2-1
Quarter-Final	Real Zaragoza	2-0	0-2	2-2
	Rangers won on the toss of a coin			
Semi-Final	Slavia Sofia	1-0	1-0	2-0
Final	Bayern Munich	—	—	0-1
1969-70				
Round 1	Steaua Bucharest	2-0	0-0	2-0
Round 2	Gornik Zabrze	1-3	1-3	2-6

Stage	Opponents	Home	Away	Agg
1971-72				
Round 1	Rennes	1-0	1-1	2-1
Round 2	Sporting Lisbon	3-2	3-4	6-6
	Rangers won on away goals			
Quarter-Final	Torino	1-0	1-1	2-1
Semi-Final	Bayern Munich	2-0	1-1	3-1
Final	Moscow Dynamo	—	—	3-2
1973-74				
Round 1	Ankaragucu	4-0	2-0	6-0
Round 2	B Moenchengladbach	3-2	0-3	3-5
1977-78				
Preliminary	Young Boys Berne	1-0	2-2	3-2
Round 1	Twente Enschede	0-0	0-3	0-3
1979-80				
Preliminary	Lillestrom	1-0	2-0	3-0
Round 1	Fortuna Dusseldorf	2-1	0-0	2-1
Round 2	Valencia	1-3	1-1	2-4
1981-82				
Round 1	Dukla Prague	2-1	0-3	2-4
1983-84				
Round 1	Valletta	10-0	8-0	18-0
Round 2	Porto	2-1	0-1	2-2
	Rangers lost on away goals			

INTER-CITIES FAIRS/UEFA CUP

Rangers have rarely participated in this competition for 'best runners–up'. Here's how they've fared to date.

Stage	Opponents	Home	Away	Agg
1967-68				
Round 1	Dynamo Dresden	2-1	1-1	3-2
Round 2	Cologne	3-0	1-3	4-3
Round 3	Bye			
Quarter-Final	Leeds United	0-0	0-2	0-2
1968-69				
Round 1	Vojvodina	2-0	0-1	2-1
Round 2	Dundalk	6-1	3-0	9-1
Round 3	DWS Amsterdam	2-1	2-0	4-1
Quarter-Final	Atletico Bilbao	4-1	0-2	4-3
Semi-Final	Newcastle United	0-0	0-2	0-2
1970-71				
Round 1	Bayern Munich	1-1	0-1	1-2
1982-83				
Round 1	Borussia Dortmund	2-0	0-0	2-0
Round 2	Cologne	2-1	0-5	2-6
1984-85				
Round 1	Bohemians	2-0	2-3	4-3
Round 2	Inter Milan	3-1	0-3	3-4

RANGERS

Stage	Opponents	Home	Away	Agg
	1985-86			
Round 1	Osasuna	1-0	0-2	1-2
	1986-87			
Round 1	Ilves Tampere	4-0	0-2	4-2
Round 2	Boavista	2-1	1-0	3-1
Round 3	B Moenchengladbach	1-1	0-0	1-1
	Rangers lost on away goals			
	1988-89			
Round 1	Katowice	1-0	4-2	5-2
Round 2	Cologne	1-1	0-2	1-3
	1997-98			
Round 1	RC Strasbourg	1-2	1-2	2-4
	Entered after eliminated from European Cup			

Rangers' record against European opposition					
Country	**P**	**W**	**D**	**L**	**F-A**
Austria	2	2	—	—	3-0
Belgium	6	4	1	1	13-8
Bulgaria	4	3	—	1	6-4
Cyprus	2	1	1	—	1-0
Czechoslovakia	6	3	1	2	9-10
Denmark	2	2	—	—	3-0
East Germany	4	3	1	—	9-4
Eire	6	4	1	1	18-6
England	10	3	3	4	11-15
Faroe Islands	2	2	—	—	11-0
Finland	2	1	—	1	4-2
France	17	5	5	7	24-30
Germany (inc West)	31	9	12	10	42-45
Greece	2	—	—	2	0-3
Holland	11	5	2	4	14-16
Hungary	2	1	—	1	5-4
Italy	14	4	1	9	12-27
Malta	4	4	—	—	28-0
Northern Ireland	2	1	1	—	5-1
Norway	2	2	—	—	3-0
Poland	6	3	1	2	11-10
Portugal	6	4	—	2	11-9
Romania	6	2	2	2	5-5
Russia	7	5	1	1	16-6
Spain	12	4	1	7	13-20
Sweden	2	—	1	1	1-4
Switzerland	6	2	2	2	6-8
Turkey	2	2	—	—	6-0
Yugoslavia	7	3	1	3	11-11

SUBSTITUTES

The arrival of substitutes in the mid 1960s, initially as insurance against injuries, changed the way football was played. Tactical matters would soon loom large.

Rangers' first sub in a League game was Jim Millar, who replaced centre-forward Gerry Forrest in an October 1966 game against Falkirk at Ibrox. The replacement could hardly have been a tactical one, since the Bairns were on the wrong end of a 5-0 scoreline that day!

Only eight substitutes were used throughout that season in League games, that figure rising to 14 in 1967-68. Davie White, in his one full term in charge, used Alex Ferguson as his secret weapon, and the future Manchester United manager came out of 1968-69 with the fascinating figure of seven starts, five substitute appearances and six goals.

A similar record was registered by Graham Fyfe in 1973-74, when Jock Wallace gave him seven starts, six subs and was rewarded by six goals. But if there was a true supersub in the 1970s it was Derek Parlane, brought on 16 times in 1977-78 to add his firepower to a Championship season.

Other Rangers to get into double figures from the bench included Gordon Smith (10 in 1979–80), Ian Redford (12 in 1981–82), John MacDonald (16 in 1983–84) and Robert Russell (10 in 1985–86). Davie Cooper spent two seasons warming the bench as Graeme Souness reshaped his team, registering 26 sub appearances to 30 starts between 1987 and 1989. Putting a player on like that with fresh legs often spelled torment for tiring defenders, so who could say he was wrong in conserving such an asset?

Mark Walters was used in similar fashion later in Souness's reign, as was Lexi Mikhailichenko under Walter Smith. Even the biggest names haven't been excused a spell of bench duty: Ally McCoist enjoyed – no, that's hardly the word – a long spell on the sideline when he fell out with Graeme Souness, while 1997–98 saw Paul Gascoigne kept up Walter Smith's sleeve for periods. It's rumoured he thought about practising a musical instrument to while away the idle hours…but that's another story entirely!

DREAM TEAM 3

The team that brought the Treble to Ibrox for the most recent time in 1992–93 was a creation of several countries. We spotlight Walter Smith's international brigade.

GORAM
1

McCALL 2
McPHERSON 5
GOUGH 4
ROBERTSON 3

DURRANT 7
BROWN 6
MIKO 8
HUISTRA 11

McCOIST 9
HATELEY 10

Goalkeeper   **Andy Goram**

Footballer of the Year and rightly so, Goram laid the Jimmy Greaves jest about Scottish goalkeepers to rest once and for all as he laid the foundations for the 1992-93 Treble. Missed six League games all told.

Right-back   **Stuart McCall**

Midfielder pressed into service as an emergency full-back with Scott Nisbet injured, the Yorkshire-born Scots international responded superbly. Has worn every shirt at Ibrox except 1 and Laudrup's 11.

Left-back   **David Robertson**

Now with Leeds, Robertson proved good value for a near £1 million fee set by tribunal as he arrived from Aberdeen. Highly consistent, he made his Scotland debut in 1992 against Northern Ireland but the subsequent dearth of caps is baffling.

Central defender   **Richard Gough**

Gough's sixth season as a Ranger saw him raise yet more silverware, and, had it not been for losing the following season's Cup Final to Dundee United by just one goal, would have become the first Gers skipper to achieve the double Treble.

Central defender   **Dave McPherson**

His first season back after five with Hearts saw the born-again Ranger record an impressive 80 per cent attendance record at the heart of the defence, but after another full campaign he found himself back at Tynecastle in part-exchange for Alan McLaren.

Midfielder   **John Brown**

Played more games than anyone this term, but would never have become a Ranger in the first place had not a move from Dundee to Hearts fallen through for medical reasons. Whole-hearted player who'd move on to the coaching staff.

Midfielder   **Ian Durrant**

A local lad who nevertheless thrived as Rangers recruited from far and wide, he was on his way back from serious injury, playing 11 of his 30 games as substitute.

Midfielder   **Alexei Mikhailichenko**

Ukraine international 'Miko' became a firm fan favourite despite refusing to be interviewed in English and shunning the off-field limelight. On his day he could be a class act, scoring 20 goals from midfield over his first three seasons.

Centre-forward   **Ally McCoist**

Mr Goals himself, the boy from Bellshill filled his boots between 1991 and 1993, scoring 68 times in 72 appearances over those seasons. A broken leg would halt that hot streak, but during this period he was simply unstoppable.

Centre-forward   **Mark Hateley**

This campaign and the previous saw the 'Coisty-Hateley' dream team notch up 108 League goals between them. The big Englishman played on through initial fan abuse to prove himself indispensable.

Winger   **Pieter Huistra**

A tricky Dutch international winger, Huistra repaid his modest £300,000 fee and would have done more but for the European problem of limiting non-Scots. Did well domestically over five seasons at Ibrox before moving to Japan.

WORST SEASON 3

The 1985–86 campaign was the only season in Rangers' history they failed to average at least a point from each match played. Their fifth position in the League was their worst performance since 1964–65.

No surprise, then, that it saw the departure of Jock Wallace, a man who, having taken Rangers to the European Cup Winners' Cup and bagged two Trebles in three seasons, made the fatal mistake of returning to relive past glories. After managing Leicester and Motherwell, he inherited a team that under John Greig had been long on the wane, and, despite a pair of back-to-back League Cup wins, was unable to re-establish Rangers as Championship contenders.

This season saw them lose the chance of the League Cup hat-trick in the last of the competition's two-leg Semi-Finals against Hibs. Hearts completed an Edinburgh double when they knocked them out of the FA Cup, and unfancied Spaniards Osasuna ended their UEFA Cup interest, both the latter at the first hurdle. In the League only McCoist made it into double figures, his 25 goals just three behind the aggregate of all the other players.

Embarrassing moments included consecutive home defeats to Dundee, Aberdeen and Hibernian, failing to score against Clydebank, also at Ibrox, and a brace of away defeats at St Mirren, the latter after Wallace's departure.

Ex-Clydebank striker Bobby Williamson failed to set the world alight up front, while goalkeeper Nicky Walker found himself back in the reserves the following season – though he would come back to play for Scotland while with Hearts. Ultimately, though, few players could avoid sharing some of the blame for a dismal campaign.

When the only bright spot of the season is beating Celtic in the Glasgow Cup (3–2, inevitably a McCoist hat-trick) you can be said to have had a tough time. With power having changed hands in the boardroom, it was no surprise when Graeme Souness was called back from Italy in April to give Ibrox the kiss of life.

1985–86 LEAGUE RECORD		
Opponents	**Home**	**Away**
Aberdeen	0-3	0-1
Aberdeen	1-1	1-1
Celtic	3-0	1-1
Celtic	4-4	0-2
Clydebank	0-0	1-0
Clydebank	4-2	1-2
Dundee	0-1	2-3
Dundee	5-0	1-2
Dundee United	1-0	1-1
Dundee United	1-1	1-1
Hearts	3-1	0-3
Hearts	0-2	1-3
Hibernian	1-2	3-1
Hibernian	3-1	1-1
Motherwell	1-0	3-0
Motherwell	2-0	0-1
St Mirren	3-0	1-2
St Mirren	2-0	1-2

IBROX'S ALL-TIME ROLL OF HONOUR

1876-77	FA Cup Runners-up
1878-79	FA Cup Runners-up
1890-91	Division One Champions (shared with Dumbarton)
1893-94	FA Cup Winners
1896-97	FA Cup Winners
1897-98	FA Cup Winners
1898-99	Division One Champions, FA Cup Runners-up
1899-1900	Division One Champions
1900-01	Division One Champions
1901-02	Division One Champions
1902-03	FA Cup Winners
1903-04	FA Cup Runners-up
1904-05	FA Cup Runners-up
1910-11	Division One Champions
1911-12	Division One Champions
1912-13	Division One Champions
1917-18	Division One Champions
1919-20	Division One Champions
1920-21	Division One Champions, FA Cup Runners-up
1921-22	FA Cup Runners-up
1922-23	Division One Champions
1923-24	Division One Champions
1924-25	Division One Champions
1926-27	Division One Champions
1927-28	Division One Champions, FA Cup Winners
1928-29	Division One Champions, FA Cup Runners-up
1929-30	Division One Champions, FA Cup Winners
1930-31	Division One Champions
1931-32	FA Cup Winners
1932-33	Division One Champions
1933-34	Division One Champions, FA Cup Winners
1934-35	Division One Champions, FA Cup Winners
1935-36	FA Cup Winners
1936-37	Division One Champions
1938-39	Division One Champions
1946-47	Division One Champions, League Cup Winners
1947-48	FA Cup Winners
1948-49	Division One Champions, FA Cup Winners, League Cup Winners
1949-50	Division One Champions, FA Cup Winners
1951-52	League Cup Runners-up
1952-53	Division One Champions, FA Cup Winners
1955-56	Division One Champions
1956-57	Division One Champions
1957-58	League Cup Runners-up
1958-59	Division One Champions

1959-60	FA Cup Winners
1960-61	Division One Champions, League Cup Winners, European Cup Winners' Cup Runners-up
1961-62	FA Cup Winners, League Cup Winners
1962-63	Division One Champions, FA Cup Winners
1963-64	Division One Champions, FA Cup Winners, League Cup Winners
1964-65	League Cup Winners
1965-66	FA Cup Winners, League Cup Runners-up
1966-67	League Cup Runners-up, European Cup Winners' Cup Runners-up
1968-69	FA Cup Runners-up
1970-71	FA Cup Runners-up, League Cup Winners
1971-72	European Cup Winners' Cup Winners
1972-73	FA Cup Winners
1974-75	Division One Champions
1975-76	Premier Division Champions, FA Cup Winners, League Cup Winners
1976-77	FA Cup Runners-up
1977-78	Premier Division Champions, FA Cup Winners, League Cup Winners
1978-79	FA Cup Winners, League Cup Winners
1979-80	FA Cup Runners-up
1980-81	FA Cup Winners
1981-82	FA Cup Runners-up, League Cup Winners
1982-83	FA Cup Runners-up, League Cup Runners-up
1983-84	League Cup Winners
1984-85	League Cup Winners
1986-87	Premier Division Champions, League Cup Winners
1987-88	League Cup Winners
1988-89	Premier Division Champions, FA Cup Runners-up, League Cup Winners
1989-90	Premier Division Champions, League Cup Runners-up
1990-91	Premier Division Champions, League Cup Winners
1991-92	Premier Division Champions, FA Cup Winners
1992-93	Premier Division Champions, FA Cup Winners, League Cup Winners
1993-94	Premier Division Champions, FA Cup Runners-up, League Cup Winners
1994-95	Premier Division Champions
1995-96	Premier Division Champions, FA Cup Winners
1996-97	Premier Division Champions, League Cup Winners

QUIZ ANSWERS

See page 124–127 for questions.

1. 'Ready'

2. Graeme Souness

3. Ray Wilkins

4. Perugia

5. Norwegian

6. Jock Wallace

7. Terry Hurlock

8. Stirling Albion

9. Third

10. David Murray

11. Archibald Leitch

12. RC Strasbourg

13. Chris Woods

14. Richard Gough

15. Scot Symon

16. Alex Ferguson

17. Willie Johnston

18. Vienna

19. One

20. One

21. Gary Stevens

22. John Greig

23. Trevor Steven

24. Because of the Hampden Riot

25. Ally McCoist

26. Dumbarton, after a 2–2 draw in a play-off match

27. Israeli

28. Hearts

29. Serbian

30. Newcastle United

31. Steven Pressley

32. Four

33. Davie Cooper

34. Paul Gascoigne

35. Leeds

36. Derek Johnstone

37. Terry Butcher

38. 1987–88

39. None

40. Gordon Durie

THE LAST WORD

'Rangers fans expect
the team to win every match,
every competition...'

Walter Smith